IF

IF

Zophia,
Thank you so much!! For your friendship & support & patience & for everything. I hope you are doing well, & hope you enjoy the book!!
Ingrid Pritchard Wilder

INGRID PRITCHARD
WILDER

NEW DEGREE PRESS

IF

ISBN   978-1-63676-697-3   *Paperback*

          978-1-63730-467-9   *Kindle Ebook*

          978-1-63730-468-6   *Ebook*

To my family, both DNA-related and otherwise.

*Thank you for loving me more than any one
person has the right to expect to be loved.*

Most of all, to my big sister Maren.

*Thank you for being my role model, my mentor, my biggest fan,
and my best friend. I've written over sixty-five thousand words
for this book, but right now I'm sitting here, frozen, because I
can't think of any words that might show how grateful I am to
have you as a sister. I love you a ridiculous amount. Also, I'm
sorry I hit you with my bike that time when we were kids.*

*I love you all very much. I can't imagine
where I'd be if I didn't have you.*

TABLE OF CONTENTS

———

PROLOGUE   9

CHAPTER 1.   IF HARRISON WAS SINGLE, I'D STILL
             HAVE MY DIGNITY (AND MY SCONE)   15

CHAPTER 2.   IF I HAD TAKEN THE STAIRS THIS
             MORNING, I WOULD KNOW THE
             MEANING OF LIFE BY NOW   31

CHAPTER 3.   IF I HAD A KEURIG, I WOULDN'T HAVE
             DISAPPOINTED MY MOTHER TODAY   51

CHAPTER 4.   IF KIDS THESE DAYS WOULD LOOK
             UP FROM THEIR DAMN CELL PHONES,
             I WOULD NOT HAVE BEEN AMBUSHED
             BEHIND A TREE   69

CHAPTER 5.   IF I HAD REMEMBERED TO EAT DINNER,
             CHASE WOULD STILL HAVE HIS SHOES   81

CHAPTER 6.   IF I HADN'T HAD THOSE EXTRA
             ESPRESSO SHOTS, I WOULDN'T HAVE
             MADE IT THROUGH THE DAY   91

CHAPTER 7.   IF DORM ROOMS HAD BALCONIES, I
             COULD HAVE AVOIDED HIM   105

CHAPTER 8.   IF I HAD DITCHED CLASS, I WOULDN'T
             HAVE ENDED UP IN THAT ALLEY   113

CHAPTER 9.   IF I WERE A LIBRA, I WOULD BE
              GETTING LAID TONIGHT   125

CHAPTER 10.   IF I HAD GOTTEN LAID LAST WEEKEND,
              I WOULDN'T BE STUCK IN
              AN ELEVATOR NOW   143

CHAPTER 11.   IF I HAD DONE YOGA INSTEAD OF
              JOURNALING, I WOULD NEVER HAVE
              GOTTEN MY MEMORIES BACK   165

CHAPTER 12.   IF CHASE HADN'T BEEN WEARING HIS
              GUCCI BELT, I COULD HAVE ESCAPED
              BEFORE THE WHOLE MONOLOGUE   179

CHAPTER 13.   IF ONLY THE GOOD DIE YOUNG, WHAT
              DOES THAT MAKE ME?   195

CHAPTER 14.   IF I HAD JUST FLIRTED WITH SOME
              DIPLOMATS, I WOULDN'T BE
              ABOUT TO DIE   209

CHAPTER 15.   IF I SURVIVE THIS—   227

CHAPTER 16.   IF—   241

              EPILOGUE   253

              ACKNOWLEDGMENTS   259

PROLOGUE

———

SUMMER, 2023

"I thought you were dead, you know."

I knew the unkempt man across the table was talking to me. All the other patients had long since retreated to their rooms to sleep, which left only the two of us under the supervision of an uninterested nurse.

Still, I didn't look up from my Jell-O.

I didn't want to talk to this man, or any of the other patients here. I didn't want to learn names, share traumas, or swap stories about what's wrong with us. *Or, at least, I wouldn't want to if I knew what was wrong with me.*

So, I poked tiny forkfuls of my neon green dessert and tried to lose myself in a well-worn novel I had grabbed from the ward's meager book collection.

He didn't seem to notice my lack of interest though, or perhaps he simply didn't care.

"When those doctors wheeled you in here," he went on, even as I held my book up higher to barricade my face from his view, "you were *so* still. Like, not even breathing. I thought you were a goner for sure. But then they left you in that room at the end of the hall, and an hour later you poked your head out the door, alive as ever. You looked timid as hell, mind you, but alive."

I turned a page aggressively, even though I hadn't actually managed to read anything on the prior page. I didn't remember the entrance he described; I had no way of knowing if it was true.

I had been on summer break, enjoying the sun and the city, the time off before college started and Chase and I went long distance, and then...

I remembered a harsh fluorescent light—too bright, like someone scrubbing bleach in my eyes. I remembered stumbling out of a bed onto a frozen tile floor, feeling exposed underneath a thin cotton hospital gown. I remembered that I was alone.

Where are you, Chase? I repeated this question and a thousand others, over and over again in my diary. Or, I would have, if my diary wasn't absent too. *I* had *had a diary, right?*

"Most people, when they come in here," continued the man, who had somehow *still* not given up, "they're kicking or screaming or fighting, or at least, doing something. I've been here three weeks, and I don't think I've seen any check-in so quiet before. 'Course, I know some of them come into the hospital that way, if it's pills or something, but usually the other doctors have to fix them up a little before they're brought in here."

"It wasn't pills."

I probably shouldn't have said that.

For one thing, the only evidence I actually had that it wasn't pills came from my panel of therapists and the story my parents had relayed through gasping sobs. I had nodded along. I cried with them, but no matter how hard I tried, I couldn't remember the event.

For another, it really should not have mattered whether this man thought I overdosed. After I was released, I would never think about him or any part of this experience again. I was going to move forward with my life and rip this horrid chapter from my narrative.

Don't engage, my mom would have said. *Just ignore him.*

But the man had already pounced hungrily on my mistake. He moved around the table, his chair scraping angrily on the floor, and roughly pulled my book away.

I looked to the nurse for help, but he had tuned us out entirely in favor of whatever video was playing on his phone. I thought briefly about punching the other patient to make him shut up, but I didn't actually think I could beat him in a fight. This man had at least half a foot and twenty years on me. *Hmm... When I get out of here, I should start lifting.*

Besides, even *if* I thought I could win a fight, my favorite doctor had told me that if I kept my head down and finished my treatment, I would be released in just a few days. Fighting another patient probably didn't qualify as keeping my head down.

"So, what are you doing here, then?" he urged.

I glared at the man frostily, which he somehow misinterpreted as a request to keep talking.

"Well, come on," he said matter-of-factly, as though we were working through a difficult multiple-choice question, and he was helping eliminate the answers that were obviously wrong. "You're not a total loner; I've seen gift baskets from your friends piling up at the front desk. You're clearly well off; your parents have been visiting every day now, and even *I* can tell their clothes are expensive. And besides," he concluded, reaching forward to stroke a strand of blonde hair that had fallen into my face, "you're *so* pretty."

His touch made me want to throw up.

I could feel the man's hot breath on my face, and it smelled like the mystery casserole I had avoided at dinner. Worse, I could feel his expectation—his confident assumption that I would provide a simple reason for my stay here in the Wollstone University Hospital Psychiatric Ward, like a neat little bow he could use to tie up my story.

Spoiled rich girl parties at one too many clubs, goes on a bender.

College freshman sleeps with one too many frat boys, falls off the deep end.

I didn't have a simple answer though, for him or for myself.

On some level, I had been depressed since middle school. When I started high school, everything felt worse, or at least more overwhelming. It didn't feel like I was growing up—not exactly. It was abrupt. My life seemed to slingshot from one moment to the next, forcing me to tumble forward in time without ever quite stopping so I could figure out who I was supposed to be or what I was meant to do.

If, as this man thought, I could have made some friends and smiled away my depression, then I would be fine. If there was a way to prepare or research or buy my way into good mental health, then my parents, who ran the hospital we were sitting in, would have done it already. They would have done anything.

And if I could have erased my pain with pretty makeup as easily as I could erase the dark circles under my eyes, then that pain would be gone, along with the memories of waking up in front of five doctors while they informed me that I had tried to jump.

I had tried to jump. Maybe that was as close to a simple answer as I would ever get.

"Hey! What are you two doing?" The nurse finally noticed the man hanging over me.

"We were just talking," the patient whined, but he had already picked up his chair to move hastily away from me. *Thank God.*

"*I* was just reading," I said, trying to separate myself from any admonishment that might come.

The nurse narrowed his eyes. "You should both go to bed."

No. Wait.

"I was *just reading*," I repeated, desperation coloring my words. "I'm not tired yet."

He was unmoved. "I'll give you something to help you sleep. It's late." He walked back to reception to get the sedative, ignoring my protests.

The other patient was quietly laughing at my panic. "Why don't you want to go to bed? Afraid of the dark?"

I didn't bother to respond. Instead, I jumped up, threw my half-eaten Jell-O in the nearest trash can with a little more force than necessary, and followed the nurse.

"Okay," I told him using my best impression of a casual tone. "You're right, I'm tired. Goodnight!"

"Wait." My path was blocked by light blue scrubs. The nurse looked down at me, and his eyes narrowed as he scrutinized my face, as if my lie was written across my forehead in bright ink. "I still think you should take this," he said, and he handed me a pill and a small cup of water.

"Okay!" I repeated, taking both. I tried to walk quickly back to my room.

"No!" The order echoed down the hallway. "Take it here, in front of me."

Shit. I turned, slowly, and he was watching me, face full of suspicion. *Shit, shit, shit.* If I argued, he would tell my doctors, and I would be trapped for even longer.

I had to take it. I had to sleep. I had to face the dreams again.

I slowly brought my hand to my lips and swallowed the pill, hating the way it felt chalky on my tongue before I chased it with the water. I glared at the nurse the entire time.

"Goodnight," I said cooly. He nodded, dismissing me to my room.

***

I laid on my stiff mattress and fought to stay awake for as long as I could. *Maybe tonight will be the first night the dreams don't come,* I tried to reassure myself.

But I knew it was no use. It seemed that barely any time had passed before I was numb, warm, and comfortable, and the drug and the dreams started to pull my mind away.

There was nothing left to do but give in and try to make it through the night. For now, my nightmares would overtake me, but tomorrow morning the sun would rise, and I would begin to run from them again.

CHAPTER ONE

IF HARRISON WAS SINGLE, I'D STILL HAVE MY DIGNITY (AND MY SCONE)

──────

FALL, 2023

Above us, clouds hung dark and heavy, ready to descend into the warm air of the early autumn evening. Below us, rubber boots touched ancient brick as we stood huddled together in the center of the square.

My college roommate, Emilia, was wearing a big blue rain jacket that looked like it could have kept a Titanic passenger dry. She had brown hair hung loose above her shoulders and oversized round glasses perched on the bridge of her nose, just above where a scrape was still healing from the previous weekend. Exactly *how* she cut her nose open was a little fuzzy. That moment sat precariously, near the edges of my memory. If I tried to reach it, it began to fade away.

It definitely happened while we were walking home from a party across campus, dizzy from the laughter and the drinks. It was probably sometime after I threw up all over the historic front steps of Gotland Hall. It may have had something to do with a tree.

"Where are the boys?" Emilia asked. She flung her arms out in frustration, nearly knocking me over. "Oops, sorry! But I'm hungry, and I think it's about to rain."

We had been waiting for at least ten minutes among the falling leaves and chatting students of Lynum Square, but I didn't mind. I loved days like this. The campus was dotted with the first decorations of fall: pumpkins and vibrant wreaths placed here and there, the smell of cinnamon spilling through the air. My classmates looked so cozy in their autumn attire, with boys in fitted sweaters with collared shirts and girls in thigh-high socks and houndstooth coats. The storm rolling in overhead tied the whole scene together with an electric buzz, like something exciting might blow in on the next gust of wind. If I squinted, I could almost believe that the timeworn stone turrets and ivy-covered walls around me belonged to a haunted castle rather than a party school.

A group of girls I vaguely recognized from my Perplexities of Theology lecture walked past us, calling out a greeting as they went.

I grinned and waved back, but as soon as they were gone I turned to my roommate. "Do you remember any of their names?" I whispered.

"Will would know," Em murmured back, zipping up her coat as the wind picked up a little speed. "He knows everyone's name, he's got, like, a perfect memory."

"That doesn't help us if he's not actually here though," I said sadly. *I would kill for a memory like that.* "The boys are all in that seminar 'Cults of the US' on Monday evenings, right? Maybe the professor is holding them back late; I heard she's super strict."

"In that case, she should have to feed us."

"Oh! I still have half a scone from Company in my backpack," I remembered. "It's yours if you want it."

"Chocolate chip?"

I clutched my heart and made a show of looking offended. "As if you have to ask. You really think I would buy one of the ones with fruit baked in? I hate those. It's, like, food can be healthy, or it can be a pastry. Trying to do both is just reaching too far."

"Some people think the baked-in fruit tastes *good*," Em protested.

"And I hope to God I never meet those people."

I crouched down to unzip my bag, landing in a precarious but well-practiced balance on my tiny black heels. I felt my skirt brush the ground as I searched for the scone and prayed that it hadn't picked up a stain. It was my favorite skirt, emerald and pleated and so short that if my mother saw it, she might invoke my middle name. It was also one of the few remaining pieces of clothing I hadn't ruined somehow in my two months of college.

There was something special about the dust that had collected at Wollstone over the past two and a half centuries. It was different from other old places; it could latch on to you and never let go. I had found this out the hard way, after I scratched a pair of pumps while climbing the iconic statue of school founder Ignatius Leahy on a dare and permanently stained a brand-new dress while hooking up with a pretty girl in a secret passageway.

Wollstone University had been founded by the Jesuits in Washington, DC, a few years before the founding of the country around it. Two and a half centuries later, it was still just as grand and intimidating as most ancient Catholic things. The school seemed to know when you passed through important places and touched famous things. It saw you as you walked over founding fathers' footsteps. It witnessed every path you wore. For every mark you made on Wollstone, Wollstone made a mark on you.

The grounds were still traversed by presidents and princes, celebrities and socialites. Some of them were students, but others came for lectures, conferences, and clandestine meetings with our famous professors. It also didn't hurt that Wollstone was located in DC, so kings and queens could wander through on their way to the White House, enjoying the tulip gardens and Gothic architecture before they went to finalize a treaty.

But the visiting dignitaries never seemed to get as dirty as I did. Maybe it was because those who ran the world stayed on the path; they never lounged on the lawn or explored underground tunnels. But somehow it felt more personal than that. Some obnoxious instinct insisted that I collected so much dust because the university *knew* I didn't belong there, posing among the prestigious. I hadn't earned my place, not yet. *But maybe someday.*

"Ivy!" Emilia huffed, with a volume and tone that made me think it wasn't her first attempt to get my attention.

I shook my head, pushing the inner whispers of *imposter* to the back of my brain and refocusing on the present.

"Sorry," I said sheepishly, as I stood up and gave her the scone. "I was lost in thought."

"I could tell," said Emilia, taking a bite of the scone. "I was just saying," she continued, her words muffled by a mouthful of pastry, "that I hope the boys have been kidnapped. Or murdered. Or possibly kidnapped and then murdered."

They weren't that late, were they? I checked the watch draped around my left wrist, before remembering that the battery had died weeks ago. *Hmm. I should probably fix that.*

Loud, low-pitched barking echoed throughout the square, and I looked up to see what was making the noise. I saw a mountain of golden fluff moving toward us, tugging a woman in a brown tweed coat along after him.

"Can I pet your dog?" The words flew out of my mouth as I ran across the quad.

The woman had thick glasses and chalk-stained hands, so I guessed she was a professor. She gave me a nod and a radiant smile, and I dove down to dog-height quickly so I wouldn't see Emilia rolling her eyes.

"Can we *please* get a dog?" I asked Em, smiling at the feel of my hand passing through fur.

"We have a cactus!" called my roommate.

"That died three weeks ago," I countered.

I had never had a dog before, or any other pet. I wanted one for Christmas when I was a kid but my mom, who possessed ninety-five percent of the common sense for my entire family, had pointed out that my dad and I would forget to feed it or walk it or clean up its poop, leaving her stuck taking care of the animal all by herself.

She was right, of course—my mom was right a ridiculous amount of the time—but that hadn't stopped five-year-old Ivy from feeling heartbroken at her lack of a furry friend. So, my mom, Astrid Bell, who would be on the cover of *Time* if they had a feature for "Busiest Woman Alive," somehow found time to go to *eleven* toy stores so she could track down a robotic toy gerbil to give me in place of a real pet. It was my favorite Christmas gift.

"What about a fish?" Em countered my suggestion as I finally tore myself away from the dog.

"Thank you! Have a lovely day!" I called after the professor as she walked away before pinching my eyebrows together in thought. *Hmm.* A fish could be pretty, but I wanted something you could hug. "What about a cat?"

"What if someone on our floor's allergic?"

Shoot, that was a good point.

"A bird?"

Emilia made a face. "I'm scared of birds. They shouldn't be able to fly *and* peck. That's, like, way too dangerous. They should only be allowed to do one."

"Em, I know you're scared of birds!" I reassured her with a laugh. "That was, like, the third thing you ever told me about yourself. I was just kidding! Also, I was trying to move the negotiation away from 'fish.'"

She stuck out her tongue at me but laughed too. "How about a hamster?"

Hmm. "A snake?"

This time Em's middle finger joined her tongue. "A *hamster.*"

A hamster was good.

"Deal."

We grinned at each other, and I imagined room 603, our dorm room on the top floor of Witt Hall, filled with colorful plastic tunnels and little squeaks.

As a kid I loved my cyborg gerbil Christmas pet because it was adorable, and it could move around and squeak just like a real pet. Looking back, I loved the story because it was so totally in character for my mom. She thought five steps down the road and knew we couldn't get a dog, so she found a solution. It seemed to come naturally to her: thinking things through, solving problems, finding a way.

It didn't always come naturally to me.

Ow. I had a bad habit of chewing on my nails or lip while I thought and had absentmindedly torn a hangnail. I frowned at the blood that was now smearing onto my light pink polish, annoyed at the sting. I didn't have any bandages to cover it, but Harrison's backpack always contained half a first aid kit.

Where was he? The square was beginning to empty as students went to dinner. Cult professor or no cult professor, they should have been here by now. It was getting late, and our dining halls were so excessively bad that if we didn't get there soon there might not be anything edible left. The first people in line always took the least-disgusting food.

A shudder ran through my body involuntarily as I remembered the experimental pizza slice I'd ended up with last week, with corn kernels and boiled zucchini topping the American cheese and tomato sauce covering a gluten-free crust. To be perfectly honest, I didn't totally understand what "gluten" was, but according to the scientific observations I made of my dinner that night, it seemed to be the ingredient that differentiated a pizza crust from a pile of sand.

I pulled a chunk off the side of the scone and stuffed it quickly into my mouth, trying to suppress the memory of the way that pizza had tasted. *Don't think about bad memories, create good ones.* I couldn't un-eat the food from last week, but maybe I could avoid it tonight. *Problem solved.* Did I still have ramen noodles in my desk? There was definitely a box of Raisin Bran, but we didn't have any milk.

I searched the square again, desperate to see the boys, but didn't see them.

Oh.

Wow.

Across the square stood the most beautiful girl I had ever seen. She was framed in the brick archway that connected the Lund Institute of International Studies to Wagner Hall, balancing gracefully on her tiptoes as she taped a flyer to the wall. The girl was South Asian, with huge eyes and waves of thick black hair held back from her face by a bright red headband. Her lips were painted the same shade.

How did her lipstick look that good? When I wore red lipstick, it had this tendency to smear all over my face, no matter how recently I'd touched it up. Hers was perfect, though. *Like fire.*

Despite being smaller than I was, the girl didn't seem delicate. She seemed... *powerful.* Her friends were organized around her, facing toward her, like she was the sun and they were planets caught in her orbit. Even from here I could see how they leaned in, hanging on her every word.

And then the girl glanced up, saw me watching her, and smiled.

I really, *really* wished I hadn't still been chewing on that bit of scone. I began to choke. Loudly. I think they probably heard it on the west coast. My mind flashed to the water bottle in the side pocket of my backpack before I remembered it was actually full of coconut rum. *Get your shit together, Ivy.*

Emilia patted me on the back in a halfhearted attempt to clear my airway, but even I could see that she was really just trying not to laugh. "Are you... okay?" she asked with a small snicker.

I nodded. I coughed up the last of the crumbs and told myself I was fine, that the girl hadn't seen my near death-by-pastry. Of course, if she *had* seen it, then I was not fine and would be booking the next flight out of Dulles Airport.

I risked a glance and saw the girl and her friends, laughing about something that I could only hope wasn't me.

"Have you ever seen that girl before?" I asked, nodding to the area where she held court. I couldn't decide if she looked familiar or if I just wanted her to know me somehow.

"You have *got* to start remembering people's names, Ivy," chastised Emilia. "Or at least stop talking to so many people. You have the brain of a goldfish and the personality of a golden retriever!"

"I know, I know." I frowned, because even though I knew she was right, that didn't mean I knew to fix it. Maybe that was something I could take a vitamin for. I should ask Dr. Thana. "Do you recognize that girl, though?" *Was she in one of my classes?*

Em turned and squinted. "I've definitely seen her at a few parties." She bit her lip, thinking it over. "But no, I don't know her name or anything."

Hmm. "Do you think she saw me choking?"

"Oh my god!" My roommate's mouth fell open, and her confused look was replaced with exaggerated shock as she said, "Ivy Bell is interested in someone, during the *day*?" She put the back of her hand to my forehead and then leaned in and tried to sniff my breath as I instinctively jerked away. "Are you sober right now? You can tell me the truth."

It was my turn to roll my eyes. "I'm fine, and I'm not *interested*. She just looks familiar, that's all. I think I might have hooked up with one of her friends a couple weeks ago or something." It wasn't a great lie—I wasn't a great liar—but it was definitely like me to forget a face, and I think Emilia might have bought it for a second.

Then she sighed and shook her head at me. "Babe, you've got to stop being so weird. You always do this: you overthink everything, you spiral into a little anxiety puddle, and then you mess everything up and compensate by getting drunk and hooking up with strangers."

"I don't—" I started to object, but Em cut me off.

"You're not Bella Swan—you don't have to find true love while you're eighteen. Just… Just have a crush on someone, and don't make it a *whole thing*, okay?"

"Okay." I told myself that Em was misreading the situation, because I could totally have a crush if I wanted to. I definitely, probably could.

But when I looked back toward the archway, the girl was already walking away with her friends in tow, and I couldn't help but suck in a tiny breath of relief. It was safer my way, kissing strangers. It was safer to distract myself with someone I didn't know, didn't *want* to know. If I let myself, I could imagine what it might be like to have a real conversation with that glowing girl, imagine kissing her the way you kissed someone you really cared about, but I couldn't imagine what I would do the next day. Buy her flowers? Write her little notes with pink hearts next to her name? Fall in love?

Not again.

No, I wouldn't picture myself doing any of that. It was for the best. My life was perfect, and I wasn't going to repeat a past mistake. *I didn't need another Chase.*

Ow. I felt a headache coming on, like the kind you get from drinking an ICEE too fast. The kind I always got when I thought of that horrible boy.

Then the world lurched and spun as a pair of hands closed around my waist and lifted me into the air.

"Will!" I laughed as he twirled me in a wide circle and air whipped past my face.

The boys were finally here.

My tallest friend, Will Taylor, whirled me around in another loop before he set me back on the ground. Will was a midwestern boy who stood at least a foot taller than me. He was fair-haired and handsome in that boy-next-door kind of way—he had been a homecoming prince back at his high school in Michigan. Will was one of those popular people who seemed to know everyone on campus without ever actually trying to be well-known. He was just so genuine; it was hard *not* to like him.

"Finally! Do you think you could have taken any longer to get here?" asked Emilia, but she was laughing too.

"We totally could have," said Aiden. "It wouldn't even have been that hard."

Aiden Ricci had the personality of a stubborn cat—he was cautious and slow to warm up to strangers, but loyal and wonderful and sweet when he finally did. Aiden was from New York City, with Italian ancestry that presented itself through dark hair, thick eyebrows, and brooding features. He usually only spoke if he actually had something to say—*something* usually being a sarcastic comment or a joke about my intelligence—and when we first met, I had worried that our personalities were too polar opposite to allow for a real friendship. Thank God I was wrong.

While we were very different, it was only surface level, and not in the ways that really mattered. If Google Translate had an Aiden-Ivy setting, it would have shown that Aiden mocking me and Em for needing a stepstool in our room to reach our higher shelves was the equivalent of me giving him a hug and reminding him that I loved him. And we understood this dynamic.

"It's the heartthrob's fault we're late," Aiden continued as he pointed his thumb toward Harrison Ellis, the final member of our group. "We ran into his girlfriend."

"Ooooh!" Emilia and I gushed in unison. Harrison was the sweetest man to exist outside of a movie, and probably couldn't have hurt a fly if his life depended on it. His girlfriend, Rose, was a beautiful business major, who probably could've taken on a Fortune 500 company without breaking a sweat. Harrison and Rose had one of those pure, wonderful relationships, the kind that makes everybody else believe in love again.

"So?" I asked eagerly.

"They held hands!" yelled Will, causing Emilia and I to squeal again. "It was adorable."

"All right, come on now," Harrison replied in his easy southern drawl, smiling sheepishly. He put both hands on the back of his head and looked toward the ground, shielding his face like he did sometimes when he was embarrassed. "Let's go get dinner. It's gonna rain soon."

Sure enough, the sky had grown even darker. Somewhere in the distance came a soft growl, from thunder or maybe one of the many military helicopters that skimmed the Potomac daily. Either way, it added to the spooky atmosphere of the day, and I leaned into Will for warmth. He wrapped his jacket around me, shielding me from the wind as I pressed closer.

Emilia and I had met the boys back in August, on our first day on campus. We were balanced precariously on our beds as we hung fairy lights and photographs, desperately doing anything to make cement room number 603 feel like a home, when the three of them happened to wander past.

"You!" I cried when I spotted Will's tall frame in our hallway. "Come here, we need your help!"

That day, Harrison, Aiden, and Will learned that Emilia and I were the type of people who would invite three strangers into our room to help us decorate, even when it meant bypassing the awkward get-to-know-you phase and jumping right into friendship. In turn, we learned that they were the type of people who would accept such an offer, even when it meant helping me put all my succulents into tiny gold pots and helping Emilia hang an Argentine flag on the ceiling above her bed.

From then on, we were a group. When one of us was sick, the rest of us would email their professors and make them ramen noodles: the good kind you could buy in the "foreign" aisle at Company. When one of us had a date, the rest of us would help pick out a cute coffee shop and the perfect outfit and help clean up the mess of tried-on clothes that inevitably ended up on the floor. And, of course, when one of us was late for dinner because they had stopped to hold hands with their perfect girlfriend, we were all late for dinner.

I felt something splash against my face and glanced up only to realize that the rain had finally begun.

"We should go get inside before the storm gets worse," Emilia said, pulling her jacket tighter around her. "I saw a picture of lightning striking the Washington Monument the other day, and the Gotland Clock Tower is basically just as tall. We're basically, like, a lightning rod or something."

"We are not gonna get struck by lightning," argued Aiden, rolling his eyes. "Besides, isn't there some law that says nothing can be taller than the Washington Monument or something?"

"It might be taller," said Harrison, scrunching his face and tilting his head to the side as he examined the silhouette of

Gotland Hall against the clouds. "If you count the fact that we live on a hill."

"Exactly! And law or not, we live in a short city!" cried Emilia, looking up at Aiden. "It's not like there's a lot of tall buildings for the storm to pick."

"Oh!" I cried, bouncing on the balls of my feet. "Do you think that, when the lightning hit the monument, it, like, released the ghost of George Washington?"

Will snorted. "Wouldn't his body have to be there for that to happen?"

I shrugged and wiggled my eyebrows in mock suspicion toward the outline of the monuments just visible in the distance. "I don't know where they keep George Washington's body. Do you?"

Aiden shook his head. "Ivy, please. You do *not* need another conspiracy to investigate. Aren't you still working on the one about the secret society of midwesterners at Wollstone? And the one about the secret tunnels under the school? And the one about the CIA base underneath our dorm building?"

"Those could all totally be true!" I giggled. "There are so many rumors flying around this campus, they can't *all* be wrong. It would be weird if there wasn't a secret society somewhere on campus, even if it's not specifically that one. And I *did* find some of those old tunnels. I just haven't figured out yet if they're from the Catholics or—"

"Can we just go eat?" interjected Will. "I don't really care if the Illuminati are on our campus. I just want food."

I laughed, and the five of us set off together, away from the rain and toward Wollstone's least-objectionable dining hall. Emilia took the lead, discussing a toga party we were planning to attend this weekend with the boys, but I stayed quiet and paused a moment as we passed the archway where the beautiful girl had hung her poster.

"Apply to join the GCC!" it read in a bold font. Of course, she was in the Global Connections Coalition, Wollstone's largest student group. They were the club in charge of everything international, from inviting ambassadors to campus to running the Model UN. More interestingly, they also threw the biggest parties. At least half the students at Wollstone were members of the GCC in some capacity, and they loved to throw crazy, internationally themed ragers. Some of the themes made sense, like their famous St. Patrick's Day Shindig, where they only served Irish whiskey. Others, though, like the Roman Holiday we were currently preparing for, seemed to exist simply because someone on the board wanted to wear a toga.

Why was she hanging posters for them? Was she on the board? Freshmen were never on the board for a club that big.

I realized I didn't actually know if she was a freshman, but...

"Ivy, hurry up!" yelled Aiden, and I ran to catch my friends.

Maybe Emilia was right, and a crush, however impermanent, was a good thing. Maybe I was ready to be vulnerable again, in small steps. And maybe I should want that. After all, not everyone was Chase. At least, that's what I tried to tell myself.

I shivered as my body experienced the unpleasant jolt that always accompanied the thought of him. Emotions rolled through me, chilling and bitter, as I remembered the pain that boy had caused me. I shook my head and pushed him and all other thoughts of romance from my mind.

Emilia, my lovely and brilliant and well-meaning best friend, was entirely wrong. Beautiful people could be dangerous, and this wasn't a danger I would willingly subject myself to anytime soon. *Not again.*

There were, after all, many more enjoyable dangers, like trying the mystery goop at the dining hall pasta bar, or helping Emilia bleach her hair, or trying the new cocktail that Aiden made out of Hennessy and Capri Sun. I didn't need this danger. It was pointless, and I would let it go.

I quickened my pace to fall into step with everyone else, smiling as I felt the rain beginning to come faster. My life was fine exactly as it was, and I didn't intend to let anything—or anyone—change it.

And then the lightning struck.

And I saw him.

CHAPTER TWO

IF I HAD TAKEN THE STAIRS THIS MORNING, I WOULD KNOW THE MEANING OF LIFE BY NOW

——

Most clichés are terrible, but the worst is probably "It will all make sense in the morning."

Sure, whatever, the morning itself is fine. There's sunrise and birds chirping, and some people are into that.

But to experience the supposedly wonderful morning, I had to wake up first. I had to fight my way out of my dreams.

As far as I knew, they had started last summer in that depressing motherfu—

Don't think about it. That was before, but this is after. Your life is good now, it's perfect. You're fine.

The problem wasn't that I had the dreams, it was that I remembered them. I'd read the research Dr. Thana gave me, and the words I could comprehend amongst the complicated medical jargon said it was because of my medication, because it shorted my REM cycle. My brain had less time to sort my memories, my thoughts, my dreams. It made mistakes.

So sometimes, in the mornings, I woke up with memories that weren't memories at all but dreams I could swear were real.

It was horrible.

Had he really been there, outlined against a bolt of lightning on the edge of the campus green? It had been dark and stormy, and he had only appeared for a second, faint and far away. By the time I had truly registered what I was seeing—what I *thought* I was seeing—the lightning was gone, and so was he.

It didn't make sense that Chase, my Chase, *Chase who wouldn't even text me back all summer,* would have been standing there on my campus in Washington, DC. I must have imagined it. He was supposed to be on the other side of the country, attending classes and smoking pot at UC Berkeley. What would he have been doing here?

Of course, that question was exactly what my useless brain decided to obsess over as I dreamt that night. My mind filled with the sound of rain and thunder overlapping memories of him.

***

I was fifteen years old, clumsily stumbling down the icy brick sidewalk in three-inch heels. It was 2020, and the pandemic had just started.

The world was empty that day, as everyone holed up and hid behind their shutters. It was freezing out, and my teeth were chattering so much that I thought they might break, but I didn't care. I needed to get out of my apartment. School had shut down a week before, and I couldn't stand my own room anymore, so I had taken to wandering through DC's pastel neighborhoods.

My parents were gone all day, every day trying to hold the hospital together as the virus spread. When they were home, they were trying to hold themselves together. They drowned in the pandemic, trying to save as many people as they could, and they did a good job. They managed the highest survival rates of any hospital in the country during those months. Eventually they brought back celebrities, diplomats, even President Hillmore from the brink of death. They even saved me.

I glanced ahead and saw a boy walking toward me from the other end of the street. He looked to be about my age but was at least a foot taller than me, and he wore a light gray peacoat that hung just a little too loosely over his slender frame. The day wasn't bright, but a pair of chunky black sunglasses hung off the collar of his white V-neck.

I fought to keep my gaze from falling on the boy's face, but I was fifteen and lonely, and he was cute. Of course I looked. *Don't look like a creepy stalker, Ivy. He's going to think you're weird if you keep staring at him.*

We were approaching each other quickly, five feet apart, then three feet, then one. I angled my body to the right, trying to eliminate any chance that I might bump into him on the narrow path. My right shoe clacked against a loose brick, and I stumbled, not noticing where my left foot was going until it was too late. I felt the slide of leather on ice, and I was tipping backward toward the street.

The world began to move too fast. One second I was screaming "*Shit!*" as I hurtled toward a probable head injury. The next, two arms were wrapping around me, catching me in a tight hold. For one too-fast moment, I felt safe in his grasp. And then I realized that I was still falling.

"Whoa!"

The boy's exclamation came out in a grunt as we landed on the frozen ground in a pile of tangled limbs. His arms were still around, only now they were pinning my own to my sides, and his hands were digging painfully into my back beneath me.

His upper body was pressed into mine, and his face filled my field of vision, blocking out the street, the sky, and everything in the universe that wasn't this boy.

His eyes were framed by heavy lashes, the irises a shade of brown so dark that I might have mistaken them for black had his face not been less than an inch from my own. Above them, currently arched in surprise, was a pair of thick eyebrows, which somehow added strength to an otherwise very delicate face. His nose was thin, and his jawline was diamond sharp. His lips were, well, pretty enough to make me feel self-conscious about the fact that I was staring at his mouth.

My eyes darted back to his.

"I'm so sorry," I began, at the exact moment he said, "I was trying to catch you."

I became aware of a deep thumping sound, a heartbeat echoing throughout my body. *Was that my heartbeat or his? Could he hear it too?*

"Chase!" said the boy, his eyes darting rapidly around my face.

"What?" I blinked, trying to piece together what that had to do with his previous sentence. *God, it's cold. Was it this cold a minute ago?*

"Chase Kennedy. It's, you know, my name." His gaze centered, and now he seemed to fixate solely on my eyes.

"Oh," I said. I knew I was supposed to say something back, but all I could think about was the ice beginning to melt beneath me as my body heat leaked onto the ground. "Um, do you think we could get up now?"

Shit, that sounded rude. Why was I being so rude?

"Yeah, of course!" There was an awkward moment as the boy, *Chase*, yanked his arms out from underneath me and pushed himself up. When he was finally standing, he offered me his hand, but I had already begun to get up on my own, so he slowly pulled it back as I blushed furiously.

This was the first conversation I had had with anyone outside of my parents in a week. Why was it so awkward? Why was I being so awkward?

"Did you hit your head or anything?" asked Chase. His face was starting to pinch together in concern.

Say something. Be nice. Be... funny? "Do I seem like I have brain damage?"

Chase's mouth dropped open in horror. "No! I didn't mean—"

"I was kidding!" I interrupted, equally horrified. "I'm fine, really. I just..." How could I end that sentence?

Whenever I was anti-social around my parents' friends, my mom would wrap her arm around me and say something like, "Sorry, Ivy's exhausted! She had *three tests this week*." She would say the last part in a conspiratorial sort of stage whisper, earning me a sympathetic smile from all adults present and a free pass to be awkward for the rest of the interaction.

I didn't want to give Chase some excuse, though. I didn't particularly want to tell him the truth. I imagined my mom's charismatic voice, toning, "Sorry, Ivy's lost the ability to interact with others like a normal human being because her mental health is a complete shit-show! It started going downhill right when she entered the teen years, and she's only gotten moodier lately with the *emerging global crisis*." Although, knowing my mother, she could have sold the line.

I took a shallow breath and looked Chase in the eye. "I just didn't know exactly what to say, because you seem very nice, and I physically brought you crashing to the earth just now, which is kind of really embarrassing. I guess I was just… hoping for a second chance at the whole, you know, first-impression thing."

For a long moment my words hung frozen between us, my eyes locked upward as I tried to analyze his face through my lashes, my mouth stuck in an apologetic half-smile.

And then the tension seemed to melt. The wrinkles covering Chase's forehead disappeared as his eyebrows fell out of their worried scrunch. His lips, which had been pressed tightly together, spread out into a smile that was sweet and warm, like honey in tea.

"Do I get a name to match with the first-impression?" he asked, his head tilted in curiosity.

"That depends on what your first-impression actually is."

"Yeah?"

"Absolutely. If you're planning to remember me falling on my ass, then I'm actually a foreign princess who can't tell you my name for national security reasons. *Oh!*" I blurted, because I wasn't sure if what I had just said was actually funny, but I decided to keep piling on just in case. *That would work, right?* "I'm a foreign princess with *very* scary bodyguards, who will arrest you if you tell anyone that I tripped."

To my immense relief, he broke into laughter. "And if I don't remember you falling?"

"If you're willing to forget that," I smiled, warmth spreading through my cheeks, "then my name is Ivy Bell."

***

And then I was in my bed. Chase was gone; that day was gone. It was 2023, I was in my dorm in Witt Hall, and my sheets were knotted around me and soaked in sweat. I could already feel a headache coming on.

The Chase Kennedy that existed in my dreams was gone. Hell, so was the Ivy Bell. When we first met as fifteen-year-olds, we were both so naive and innocent, stumbling just to carry on a conversation. But that was three years ago—that was *before*. Before date nights, parties, and near death experiences.

We'd both grown up, and Chase had grown tired of me. That was just as well. I didn't miss him anymore. He didn't hurt to remember.

My past didn't matter because my present was amazing. I was at a top-tier school with amazing friends and the kind of confidence for which fifteen-year-old Ivy might have killed. Come to think of it, if someone told her my current body count, she might just have passed away on the spot.

So, it didn't matter what Chase had done or how things had ended. And it definitely, *definitely*, didn't matter that I had seen him last night, framed in a storm on the edge of my perfect campus, looking in on my perfect life.

Because that wouldn't make sense. No matter how many mornings came and went, it just wouldn't.

A beam of cloudy sunlight pushed through the blinds, nearly gouging out my eyes. I yelled "Hurrrrrmph!" into my pillow at the top of my lungs, not because it helped anything, but because I could. Emilia was my only roommate, and she wouldn't have woken from the noise if I had been yelling right into her ear.

Noise.

Music.

Alarm?

Where was my fucking alarm? How long had it been playing as I ignored it, caught up in useless memories? I swiped my hand blindly around my tangled sheets until I felt the familiar plastic of my phone's pink glitter case. I turned off the alarm, cutting off the sound Taylor Swift's peppy masterpiece, "Paper Rings," and spotted the time. *Fuck.*

I had overslept and had less than ten minutes to the start of my 8:00 a.m. Debut Philosophy and the Anomaly of the Homo Sapien class.

Why did they even have classes this early? Maybe someone in the scheduling department was a masochist. Wait, that wasn't the right word. A sadist?

Yes, that was better. Sadists like to inflict pain on others, masochists on themselves. *A sadist would tell a girl he loved her, and then abandon her in the most vulnerable moment of her life. A masochist would keep remembering that boy, even though she knew how much it hurts.*

And now he was going to make me late for class.

I forced myself out of bed and threw on sweatpants and a Wollstone tank top. I shoved blonde hair into a high ponytail and put on a swipe of mascara. I hated days like that, when I couldn't pick a cute outfit or do my makeup like I wanted. It had taken me a long time to get over my middle school "I'm not like other girls" phase and to realize that it didn't make you hollow inside to like the way you looked on the outside. Once I finally admitted to myself that I really did love makeup and pink, however, I couldn't look back. I loved getting ready in the morning and feeling put together. I could control my very appearance: the way the rest of the world perceived me. It made me feel in charge of my life, like I was more prepared to face the day.

That morning I was not in control, and I looked it. I was furious at myself for dreaming about Chase, for imagining that I saw him on my campus last night, and for letting myself oversleep because of it. I hadn't seen him in months, but I had somehow let him derail my morning.

Stupid. I wasn't fifteen anymore, and I needed to stop acting like it. *Move on. Think about something else.*

At that moment, as though the universe had heard me, a squeak sounded behind me and interrupted my spiraling thoughts. I whipped around, my arms automatically flying up into the protective crossed position ninjas use in movies. *Do they really do that in real life? Does that pose even do anything?*

It took my churning mind a few moments to process the squeak, and even longer to connect it with the small brown rat that was currently sitting on my desk. It squeaked again.

"Hello?" I asked it.

As a response, it lifted its head and wiggled its little pink nose in my direction, sniffing me. I stepped forward. It didn't run away. I reached out a hand, slowly, ready to jerk it back, but when the rat made no attempt to bite me, I gently stroked its head.

How long had it been here? Rats were everywhere in DC, including Wollstone dorms and dining halls, but I had never seen one in our room before. Was there a hole in the wall somewhere? Had it crawled in through a vent?

Focus, Ivy. You are late. You have class. You do not have time to befriend a rat.

It really was adorable, though. *It probably wouldn't even take that long to google what kind of snacks rats like.*

Three minutes later I had lined an empty White Claw box with my extra pillowcase and added a makeshift rat-ramp to the top using duct-tape and a couple of Pop-Tarts. I took a yellow banana from a stash of fruit on top of Em's desk, both because "SqueaksAndNibbles.com" said that rats liked them, and because Em only liked bananas when they were bright green like summer grass. She would have given this one away, anyway.

The rat went up the ramp into the box as soon as I put the banana chunks in. It was *so* cute. I wondered if it would still be here when I got back from class, or if it would leave the way it came. I hoped it stayed. Emilia had agreed to a hamster, and a rat was kind of the same thing. She would probably agree to this. Maybe if she said no, I could hide a little snack station for it up on the Witt rooftop and visit sometimes.

Emilia muttered something in her sleep but didn't wake up. I stuck a pink Post-It note on the inside of our door and scribbled, "Em—Found rat this morning, seems friendly, left it snacks. Cheaper than hamster?"

I crossed my fingers that she would see the note before she saw the rat, grabbed my backpack, and dashed out into the hall without stopping to lock our room. Room 603 was unlocked most of the time, anyway, because people were usually coming in and out and because, well, Emilia and I were prone to losing the keys. *Maybe a rat would scare off intruders.*

I glanced at the time on my phone, imposed over the selfie of my friends and I getting pizza at three o'clock in the morning. *Two minutes until class.* That meant I could either walk down seven flights of stairs, or I could gamble on Witt Hall's elevator, which was a million years old and would either drop violently to the ground floor in thirty seconds or creep along for ten minutes with an unnecessary stop on every other floor. The first option meant I would definitely be a little late, but the second meant I would be incredibly late *or* barely on time.

I punched the elevator button. Then I punched it three more times so that if my dorm really *was* haunted the ghost would know I meant business.

After a minute, the ancient doors slid open with a groan. I mumbled a "thank you" to any potential ghosts, dashed inside, and selected the hard plastic button labeled "M" for main. The elevator began to rattle downward with a mechanical squeal that sounded worse than when my upstairs neighbor spent his quarantine learning trombone.

All together, there were nine floors listed on the elevator's old-fashioned keypad: six through one, Main, K, and Basement. No one actually knew what "K" stood for. I had heard competing rumors that it was a tunnel to a CIA laboratory where they ran experiments on students or a solid brick wall like the entrance to Diagon Alley. Deep down, I knew it was probably a maintenance level or something, but I couldn't bring myself to believe something so boring until I knew for sure. And right now, the only thing I did know for sure was that nothing would happen if I selected the button for "K."

I pressed it anyway. *Just in case.*

I tapped my foot anxiously against the vomit-stained carpet and checked my phone. There was a text from Will and Aiden, who were both in my philosophy class, asking why I wasn't in class yet, but when I tried to text them back I received a red "no-service" error.

Was the elevator shaking, or was that just my foot?

In that moment, it seemed like there was nothing worse than the dim, flickering lights, and the sound of groaning machinery coming from the elevator. The next moment I knew I was wrong, because it was far, far worse when the lights flickered out and the machinery ground to a stop.

The floor below me wasn't moving downward anymore, but my body sure as hell still was. I landed against the carpet with a dull thump. For a moment I lay there, stunned, letting my nose fill with the carpet's scent of dirt, stomach acid, and booze.

Then logic set in, and I began to panic instead.

Oh my god. I was going to die in sweatpants.

My breathe sped up. *Was I running out of oxygen?* No, no way, it was way too early for that. *Was it?*

Or maybe my lungs weren't the problem. Maybe it was my brain.

My meds. Right now, there were little white pills for anxiety and depression in room 603, inside an old vanilla candle I'd DIY-ed to have a hidden compartment. *Did I take one before I left?* I'd been running late, moving fast, and distracted by a rodent.

Fuck, this was Chase's fault, for making me dream about him, for making me late. No, scratch that, it was *my* fault, for being stupid enough to even think about him.

I could feel my chest rising and falling, faster and faster with my stampeding lungs, but I couldn't tell if I was consuming any oxygen. *What was I supposed to do?*

I was missing something, something obvious, but I couldn't think. There was something I should do, but I couldn't quite...

Was I supposed to call someone? *The fire department, or the Air Force, or something.*

But my phone didn't have service. *Wait, elevators existed before cell phones, right? They had to.*

Oh! The elevator had a phone.

I crawled over to the wall, trying to ignore the various textures beneath my hands and knees. At least it was dark, and I couldn't see all the things that had been spilled on this carpet by decades of college students.

When I finally made it to the keypad I got to my knees shakily and blindly felt around the various buttons before landing on the emergency phone.

"Hello!" I hollered. Was the ground moving or not? Was I starting to fall?

"Hi!" A perky voice projected from the wall speaker, with a sound quality that was somehow worse than a home movie from the nineties. "This is Darlene, with Wollstone University Security! How can I help?"

"You can start the fucking elevator, Darlene!" I cried, trying to slow my breathing enough to be coherent. "I don't want to die today; I haven't even had breakfast yet!"

"Right…" Darlene responded, and there was a short burst of static. "You're trapped in the elevator in Witt Hall?"

"Yes! Please help me, Darlene!" I started to ramble, my pitch rising a little with every word. *"Please, please, please!* I'm pretty sure this carpet hasn't been replaced for decades, so what if the elevator drops too fast, and my body, like, *explodes* on impact, and then my guts soak into the carpet, and then they never change it, and then my guts are just *in* this elevator carpet forever, and—"

"Ma'am," Darlene interrupted, her tone measured and steady. "Help is on the way. You are not going to die. The elevator isn't broken. It stopped because Wollstone is experiencing a brief power outage. The backup generators should be up soon. I just need you to stay calm for a moment, okay? Can you do that for me?"

Calm. Of course, I could stay calm. Darlene was calm, and if Darlene was calm, I could be calm too, right? Wait, was Darlene *too* calm? She said help was coming, but maybe that was a rehearsed line, like telemarketers had. Maybe she wasn't supposed to say that whether or not I was about to die.

Oh god, I was going to die.

"Ma'am?" Darlene sounded like she was at the other end of a tunnel, and I was starting to see flickering spots. "Ma'am, you said it was dark. Do you have a flashlight?"

My throat felt tight, the muscles constricting. Why wasn't she helping? What kind of stupid question was that? "I'm not Nancy-fucking-Drew!" I yelled at Darlene.

"I know, ma'am." Was that a laugh? Was she laughing at me as I was about to die? Oh, I was so going to come back and haunt this woman. *What if I became the Witt Hall ghost?*

"Do you have your phone on you?" Darlene asked. "A cell phone might have a flashlight function."

Oh, right. I had my phone. I had been holding it when I fell. *Was there enough air in here?* It must be on the floor somewhere; I must have dropped it. I felt lightheaded. I tried to lean down, tried to look for my phone, but that only made me dizzier. I stumbled a little, flailing my arms out in search of something solid to hold.

"Ma'am, are you still there? I need you to breathe. Help is almost there."

"I—" Oh, the elevator was moving again, moving down. Down? Falling?

"Ma'am, the power is back on. Is the elevator working?"

Light. There was light. The elevator was slowing to a stop, and the doors were opening. I saw the Witt lobby, a Wollstone security guard, and *light*.

"Ma'am?"

"Are you the girl who was stuck?" asked the guard in a bored voice, but I didn't wait to answer him. I scrambled out of the elevator, snatching my phone and my backpack from the floor as I went, and I made a mad dash to get outside.

Fresh air.

My phone lit up as it reconnected to service. It was 8:08. I had a dozen more missed texts from Will and Aiden, but I didn't pause to answer them. I had to get away from that terrible falling death box, and suddenly there was nothing more I wanted than to reach my philosophy lecture. I sprinted through the last drizzles of yesterday's storm, cursing under my breath as I stumbled over irregular brick paths. A few students stared at me as I passed, but I told myself I didn't care.

I hated days like this, when I couldn't control anything, when the world controlled me. Days when I just wanted to wear lip-gloss and make it to class on time, but stupid boys and broken elevators got in my way.

By the time I finally got to the Lund Institute of International Studies, the pretentious looking building where my morning class met, my clothes were drenched in rain and my face was smeared with tear-stained mascara. I snuck cautiously in through a door near the back of my lecture hall, trying to muffle the squelch of my sneakers as I made my way to the seat Will and Aiden had saved for me.

In my first lucky break of the day, Professor Whitby was turned around when I reached my chair, drawing some diagram on the blackboard—Wollstone exclusively used blackboards instead of whiteboards, probably because admin thought it looked cool instead of pretentious—with the heading "Socrates" scrawled above it in dusty white chalk.

"Decided to sleep in today?" Will asked me jokingly as I sat down, which, to be fair, was a good guess in my case. But then he turned to me, and the grin on his face quickly slipped into horror. "Are you crying? You look awful. What happened?"

"Shh," whispered Aiden, who hadn't looked up from his notes yet. "Sadness is temporary, GPA is forever."

Aiden hated when we talked in class; we were entirely different types of students. He had once ripped up a photocopy of my study guide because I "used a terrible font," and "said 'lmao' too many times for a review of *Epictetus and the Stoics.*"

Still, I tried to be quiet for him. I pulled out my notebook and began scribbling in the margins for Will.

"Is it too early for me to tell you about it over drinks somewhere?" I scrawled in my favorite pink pen from my pastel set of twelve. As much as I hated taking notes, I had always hated it slightly less when I could color-code them.

"Too early in the week, or too early in the day?" Will wrote back in black ballpoint.

"Week?" I tried.

"It's Tuesday."

"Day?"

"It's 9:00 a.m."

"Shoot." I paused for a second. I didn't really want to write that I thought I had seen my ex and that the mere possibility had kept me up all night. I settled for a half truth. *"Elevator broke. Panic attack."*

"Shit, Ivy," said Will aloud, not bothering to muffle his voice. This earned him a look of annoyance from Aiden, which changed to one of concern when he saw my face. *Did I really look that bad?*

"You should have just gone back to bed," Will wrote.

"I would have if I didn't have this stupid lecture. I got a D on the last test, and if I can't do better on the final my parents might actually kill me."

Will's eyes darted over the tiny paragraph, and he nodded in understanding. Then he squeezed my hand and went back to his notes.

For the next hour, I concentrated on trying to calm my racing thoughts so that I could focus on Professor Whitby's lecture, and then, after I failed miserably, I concentrated on drawing cartoon turtles in my philosophy notebook. When the class finally ended, Aiden and Will hung back and waited for me while I went to talk to Professor Whitby at the blackboard.

"Professor?" I asked nervously.

"Yes, Miss Bell?" My philosophy professor was a young but formidable woman with wild curly hair and an accent that, as she had informed us on our first day, was from New Zealand and *not* Australia.

"I was just wondering... I mean, I wanted to apologize for being late to class, and talk about... So, the power in my dorm went off while I was in the elevator. It was the storm, I guess? And I'm not trying to sound like a coward, but it was *really* scary in there, and then I got here, and I was late, like I said before, and..." I fidgeted, anxious about why she wasn't saying anything.

"Hmm," Professor Whitby murmured, examining my still-damp clothes and flustered face. "Can I ask why you're in this class?"

Was that a trick question? "Because philosophy is a core requirement to graduate."

She laughed. "Right. I just meant that it seems like you sometimes have trouble focusing on the material."

I felt the blood drain from my face. *Was I that obvious?*

I really didn't care about this class. She was right. I had been a good student in high school, and I tried to be a decent college student too, but success here felt like an exponentially different target. It was like I had won a game of mini golf against Emilia and then advanced to the PGA Championship.

It was just so easy to get overwhelmed by all these classes, and it was even easier to just stop caring about them entirely. After all, I joined clubs, partied, and explored because it was fun, because it felt good to turn my brain off and lose focus. I studied philosophy because someone had decided, generations ago, that it was necessary to know what a bunch of dead white guys thought about the world. *Not a great reason.*

"That wasn't an admonishment," clarified Professor Whitby, interrupting my silence. "I can tell you're a bright girl, but sometimes it's hard to focus on things when we don't know why we are doing them. I think maybe you would be doing better in this class if you started with the *why*."

"Why?" *Bright girl?* I tapped my fingers anxiously on my leg as I tried to understand why she was telling me this.

"Exactly. Philosophy doesn't just mean 'wisdom,' or 'need for wisdom,' or 'enough wisdom to pass the final.' It means 'love of wisdom.'"

"Right, so you want…" I trailed off.

"If you want to gain anything from what I tell you in this room, you can't just write down what I'm saying; you have to care about why I'm saying it. You don't have to actually love it, mind you, but you have to care at least a little bit." Whitby pointed to a quote on the board.

"'Not life, but good life, is to be chiefly valued,'" I read aloud.

"Start with that quote. Don't just think about *what* a good life might be, think about *why* that life is good. You're starting college; now is the perfect time to decide what kind of life you truly value." Professor Whitby smiled and began to pack up, clearly dismissing me. "Type it up and turn it in, while you're at it," she said over her shoulder. "Maybe I can give you some extra points."

I walked away, slowly, lost in thought. I had only been here a couple of months, but even I knew it was strange for a professor to offer personalized extra credit to a single student.

Most of the professors here, though incredibly generous and well-meaning, were busy. They spent most of their time consulting on political campaigns, researching world wars, or working for the CIA. They were usually happy to get to know a student if the student reached out to them, but Professor Whitby didn't know me. I hadn't even been to her office hours before. Why would she care about giving me extra points?

"What was that?" asked Aiden as I finally reached my friends by the door of the lecture hall.

I shook my head, emptying my mind of philosophy, elevators, and lonely dreams.

"That was, like, the third weirdest thing that's happen to me this morning. Let's go get some breakfast."

CHAPTER THREE

IF I HAD A KEURIG, I WOULDN'T HAVE DISAPPOINTED MY MOTHER TODAY

———

The next week was the longest I'd had at Wollstone. During the day, it felt like my professors had made it their personal mission to wear me out with essays, pop quizzes, and a demoralizing amount of homework. At night, I kept dreaming of him.

In my dreams on Tuesday, I found myself taking long walks around the District with Chase, jumping ahead moment by moment. We walked through icy puddles playing awkward get-to-know-you games. We strolled underneath the blooming cherry blossoms wearing makeshift face masks, sharing inside jokes as pale pink petals fell in our hair. We ran through the grass at the National Mall, laughing and screaming and shooting each other with squirt guns as we tried to endure the cruel July heat.

I shrieked and covered my face to avoid a well-aimed blast of water, and when I uncovered my eyes, it was nearly three years later. We were eighteen, and he was standing so, so close to me.

"Ivy, you look..." Chase trailed off, shaking his head, but even the unspoken compliment was enough to make me blush.

"You too," I said, grinning, and I meant it. Chase had been beautiful the day I met him, but since then he had grown into himself, gotten more confident in who he was. Outdoor sports had resumed in spring of our sophomore year of high school, and he had joined the track and field team. In the fall, he'd added cross country too. Now, where he had once been lanky, he was toned, and where he had once let his hair go wild without using so much as a comb, he kept it carefully cut and styled with a product that smelled like spice. Not to mention, I had always loved a man in a tux.

"Your prom dress is beautiful," he said, and I twirled a little to show off my pink, fluffy skirt. The fabric swooshed and shimmered, and on my bodice tiny gems dotted a low, graceful neckline.

I knew that, like Chase, I looked better than I ever had. Over the past three years, I had lost the last ten pounds of baby-fat and perfected my makeup to accentuate my blue eyes and give my face an actual structure, one with cheekbones and everything. I had started to buy bras that actually fit correctly and found clothing that showed off my small waist while drawing less attention to my too-wide thighs. I had even learned cute hairstyles beyond the "blindly-throw-it-in-a-ponytail" and the "just-leave-it-down-its-fine."

We looked great. We *were* great, inside and out, and we had grown into it together. We had found the parts we loved in each other and learned how to better love ourselves.

I twirled again, and suddenly Chase and I were spinning on the dance floor, surrounded by our high school friends. The music was loud, the lights were flashing, and I was laughing, having so, so much fun. Chase's strong hands gripped my waisted and twirled me, then he dipped me horizontally, leaned down to kiss me, pressed me close. And then the dance was gone, and we were in a hotel bed. He was whispering, "Are you sure?"

I was flat on my back and he was on top of me, just like the first day we'd met. I smiled and gazed into his beautiful dark eyes. "Yeah, I'm absolutely sure." I lifted my head up, and his lips were on mine soft but sure, and then he pulled away, just for a moment, just to whisper, "I love you."

And then it was Wednesday morning, and I was late for Russian.

***

On Wednesday night, I went to bed early. I drank warm milk heated in our common room's forty-year-old microwave and downloaded a yoga app so I could stretch before I got into bed. I popped a melatonin and played "Relaxing Sleep Sounds" on YouTube. I shut my eyes.

I was in the hospital with a ventilator tube stuck down my throat.

It was 2020 again, late summer. Chase and I had both caught COVID-19. We'd been so careful, only ever interacting outside, only ever with each other. We hadn't even kissed yet.

I felt a tear fall down my face. Chase had been released so quickly. He'd had to quarantine at home, but he had been fine.

I could remember him fighting to stay in the hospital, stay with me, while security tried to force him to leave and nurses shouted that staying with me would be exposing himself to further danger from the virus.

I could remember him shouting back, screaming that it was worth it... that I was worth it.

For two weeks I was in intensive care, getting exponentially worse. At first, I had only needed a tube in my nose, then an oxygen mask, and then IVs in my arms and a ventilator.

I was tired—so, so tired.

Maybe the worst part of it all was seeing my parents standing outside the hospital room, watching their faces through glass windows as they slowly lost all hope. I had only ever seen my dad cry once before that: at his mom's funeral. He had always smiled at me before, his face had been full of the most beautiful sunshine, but now it was gone. Now he was crying every day. My mom, who always had a plan, gathered all the facts, and always found a solution, looked utterly helpless. My parents were breaking.

I blinked, hard, trying to block it all out, and when I opened my eyes again, I was lying on a metal table in a frozen steel room.

"No!" I screamed.

I jolted awake.

I was in room 603. I was healthy. It was 2023. I pushed myself to the edge of my bed, nearly toppling off the side as I tried to find the floor. I snatched my phone and room key and dashed out the door. I was already in the dorm's stairwell before I noticed I had forgotten to put on shoes.

We lived on the top floor of Witt, so it only took climbing half a flight of stairs to get to the building's rooftop. I was half expecting to have to pick the ancient lock myself, but to my surprise, the door leading outside was already propped open with a large rock.

I stepped out and passed empty glass bottles and cigarette butts. I walked into the cool night air, breathing it gratefully even as it stung my nose. *I was safe. I was healthy. It was 2023, and Chase was gone, and my life was perfect.* So why did I feel so upset?

"Are you okay?" called an unfamiliar voice.

I tensed, preparing a lie for a campus security guard. *"Do you know how to find the ladies room on the main floor? I needed to buy a tampon, and the machine in my floor's bathroom was out, and I just got so turned around that next thing you know I was up here!"*

"Hello?"

I forced my eyes to widen and turned toward the voice, armed with my prepared tampon speech. *Oh.* It was just a student.

He was sitting against the wall, only a few feet to the right of the door—I must have blown right past him in my desperation to get outside. From the small amount of light spilling out from inside, I could see that he had sandy brown hair and wore a worn-out Wollstone Men's Soccer sweatshirt. He was holding a vape pen and can of light beer, with the remains of a six-pack sitting next to him.

He noticed my gaze and gestured toward the other cans. "Want some, uh…"

"Ivy," I finished. "No thanks. I just needed to get out of my room."

"I'm Jordan," he said and brought the pen to his own lips. After a moment, he breathed out a hazy puff of air. "Couldn't sleep?"

"You could say that." I looked out past him, focusing on the DC skyline. We were too low to see the entire city, but I could catch glimpses of the National Cathedral in the distance. I felt calmer now, relaxed by the detachment from my dreams. Why had I let them freak me out so much? Why was I still living in the past?

"Why are you still awake?" I asked.

He sighed. "Long week."

I nodded. *What the hell, why not?* I walked back over to where Jordan was sitting and slid down next to him. I grabbed a can of beer, opening it with a small pop.

The rest of the night passed in peaceful silence as we sat on the roof, waiting for the sun to rise.

***

On Thursday, I didn't even bother trying to sleep. I told my friends I had to pull an all-nighter for a paper, bought a large iced mocha with three shots of espresso, and camped out in our common room instead.

By Friday afternoon that week, I was exhausted and completely over my classes. But I was so close to the weekend. All I had left was therapy, and then I was *free*. No classes, just socializing. Everything would be okay.

The Wollstone University Hospital was a massive brick building situated on the edge of campus, right next to my dorm. The walk there was only about five minutes, but it always felt much longer. It didn't matter that I had grown up visiting my parents there. It didn't even matter that we had a vaccine now and I was healthy. It still hurt to go into that building every week. My memories were like a sepia filter, changing the innocent scene before me into an eerie vision of the past.

I kept my head down as I walked past doctors and nurses in their stark white battle uniforms. I looked away from the posters that covered the hospital, posted repeatedly with the words "Stop the Spread." I tried to ignore the fact that I was stepping willingly into the place where thousands had died, where I had almost died.

My throat tightened as I stepped through the sliding doors. I bit the inside of my cheeks as I stood inside, waiting for the smiling woman at the welcome desk to confirm that my vaccines were up to date. I spoke a pained "thank you" after she finally waved me through.

It wasn't her fault, after all. She hadn't given me the virus three years ago. She hadn't admitted me to the psychiatric ward this summer. This smiling woman had no idea how close I had come to death, how terrified I still was. It wasn't her fault.

I made sure I had turned and started walking away before I let the first tear slide down my cheek. That was one of the few perks of depression: I had learned, years ago, to sob discretely and in complete silence.

No one else had to know.

By the time I got to Dr. Thana's office, my face was clear and bright. I smiled as she invited me in and sat down across from her on a soft pink chair. The room was white and lined with paintings that would make hotel room art look like an original Van Gogh.

Dr. Thana herself was pale, with red hair that she always kept pulled back in a messy bun. She wore glasses and a lab coat with shoes that clacked against the tile floor when she walked, and I had never seen her without a clipboard. I wouldn't have been shocked to learn she slept with the thing.

"I'd ask if you had gotten around to filling out your journal, but I suspect I would only be disappointed," said Dr. Thana, looking at me pointedly.

Right, I was supposed to be keeping a journal so that I could check in with myself and we could go over my thoughts together. I'd read the articles she gave me, the research about how journaling can help track mental health, but I never got around to doing it. *Oops.*

"I can see from your face that I am correct in this assumption," she said, shaking her head softly. "So, let's start with something else. How are you today, Ivy?"

I racked my brain, searching for a response that wasn't "Fine." She never liked that one. "Oh!" I said, remembering. "I got stuck in an elevator Tuesday morning."

"That sounds scary. Was it during the power outage?"

"Yeah," I responded. "How did you know there was an outage? I thought this place would have generators."

Dr. Thana nodded. "We do. However, it takes a second or two for them to power up, and I noticed a flicker that morning."

Right. Dr. Thana was so observant. She always noticed every move I made during my weekly hour in her office. Even the tiniest twitch was like a scream to her. Of course she would notice if the lights flickered.

"Is it getting easier?" she asked.

"Which part?" I nearly laughed.

Dr. Thana smiled in that patient, professional way only doctors seem to know how to do. "All of it, Ivy. It's all connected. You can't separate the pieces of your life forever; they must eventually come together. They *all* belong to you."

I resisted the urge to roll my eyes. "Right. Okay."

Is it getting easier?

In seventh grade all the students at my middle school had to sit through a health class. We pretended to take notes while our teacher, Mrs. Lewis, tried to sound enthusiastic about a PowerPoint that obviously hadn't been updated since Y2K.

Along with the repeated pleas to protect ourselves from diseases and by God *never* get pregnant, there was a brief section on mental health. We were given a list of common symptoms and treatments of anxiety, depression, and eating disorders, and then we were told that "help was available" and that "we should never feel afraid to reach out!"

I was upset that day, in that stupid, irrational way that middle schoolers are upset. It bothered me that other people got to take pills that would make them happier. It didn't seem fair. After all, I was sad all the time, but I didn't get pills to fix it. Why should they?

It was a couple of years later before it finally occurred to me I might have something in common with those frowning people in the stock photos that Mrs. Lewis projected on the board.

I dithered about it for a while. Was I really depressed, or was I just being dramatic? I didn't know what it was like in anyone else's head. Maybe they wished for pain all the time too. Maybe they had to fight to hold back tears every time the tiniest thing went wrong too.

My problems weren't any worse than anyone else's, so I told myself that it didn't make sense for me to be depressed. I didn't talk about it aloud, or even ask for help, and I told myself I was only feeling this way for the attention.

And then, in 2020, the pandemic hit. Suddenly there were bigger problems, more important things. It seemed selfish to feel so miserable all the time when people were dying.

I may have felt empty and alone inside, but I was safe. My parents still had their jobs, and I had Chase. I was fine. I was *lucky*, really, just to be able to spend so much time thinking about myself.

I pushed it down. I focused on my online classes and learning new hobbies, and when I caught the virus, I focused on that.

It was almost a relief to be sick, to be "really sick," in the traditional sense of the word. I had symptoms: visible ailments that I could point to and say, "Look! I'm in pain! It's right there. You can see it!"

I was still miserable, still empty, and still caving in on myself every day; but when I finally got sick, I had an excuse. How could I have known I would keep getting sicker?

"Ivy?" asked Dr. Thana, losing her veil of patience.

"Yes," I said abruptly. "Yes, it's getting better."

When I had made my miraculous recovery from COVID-19, I had a different outlook on life. My depression had by no means gone away, but I had come to terms with it… had finally decided it was real. I was determined, after the virus, that I would not end up back in that hospital. I had too many horrible memories there, and I would do everything in my power to keep myself safe.

I started taking care of myself in a real, productive way. I spent long nights with Chase, telling him how I felt. It was nice to have my emotions validated by someone I loved. I started exercising, not because I wanted to look better, but because I wanted to *feel* better. I even started going to a therapist, not Dr. Thana, but a nice lady who ran a private practice over in Bethesda. I really had been getting better. I was sure of it.

What happened last summer didn't quite fit in the story, though. I knew that progress wasn't linear and that it was possible to mess up, so I chose to move on and keep improving. I would not look back.

Or at least, I would try not to.

So, I smiled as genuinely as was possible to a woman who looked as impatient as Dr. Thana did and said, "Yes. It's all much better now. Absolutely."

Dr Thana tilted her head and studied my face. I knew my answer was the right one, and I had genuinely meant it, but she still wanted more.

"How's your medication working, Ivy?" she asked, finally looking away from me and instead turning toward the clipboard. "I don't see any notes in your chart about any changes."

I nodded. It was working. I hated that I had to take it, hated that I had to walk through these horrible hallways and find the pharmacy once a month, but I did it because I knew the meds really did work. They slowed down my thoughts just enough and calmed them when something was going wrong. They gave me time to really think, to consider my options and process my feelings before I spiraled to the worst possible conclusions.

"Any side effects?" asked Dr. Thana. "Aside from the dreams, of course."

"No. Just, just the dreams." I tried and failed to keep my voice neutral as I answered her question.

"What aren't you telling me, Ivy?" She challenged my failed attempt at nonchalance. "How are the dreams? Are they getting worse?"

I looked down. They had been overwhelming this week. They had been awful, but I didn't want to tell her that they had been about Chase. I didn't want to tell her that I had thought I'd seen him during a thunderstorm and then lost my mind. What if I ended up back in that stupid psych wa—

No. Don't think about that.

"Vivid dreaming is a perfectly normal side effect. There's nothing to be worried about," said Dr. Thana, her tone irked. "But you need to keep me updated so I can make sure it isn't getting out of hand. Some antidepressants simply alter your REM cycle in a way that causes your brain to process—"

"I know." That came out more harshly than I had intended. "Sorry," I said softly. "I just mean, I know about the side effect, and I know they're just dreams. I know that." I sighed. "They just... they feel so real."

She smiled sympathetically.

"Some patients—and stop me if this isn't you—but some have told me that it's hard to distinguish between dreams and memories when the dream is something that could happen in real life. For example, a zombie apocalypse is something you can wake up from and realize is just a nightmare. However, you oversleep, you miss your midterm, and you fail a class? That's a nightmare that could be real. That's when it's harder to be sure if the event in question is a dream or a memory."

Dr. Thana cleared her throat and looked at me inquisitively.

"Has that happened to you, Ivy? It's okay to be honest. I'm just trying to help you. Do you have dreams that you feel could be real?"

"I—" *Hmm.* I thought of Chase, posed dramatically in the middle of a storm. Chase, on my college campus, three thousand miles from where he was supposed to be. Chase, looking right at me after he had made it clear all summer long that he didn't intend to see me again.

Could that have been real? I thought back further, to last summer, to the day I had woken up in this very hospital with a sour taste in my mouth and a bitter outlook on love. I remembered the text I had seen when I finally got out of the psychiatric ward a few weeks later. *I'm sorry,* it read. *But you're just not worth it anymore.*

"No," I said confidently. "I have not had any dreams that I thought could be real."

***

After therapy I made the spur of the moment decision to visit my parents. I didn't have an appointment, so I knew full well that they might be busy, but I didn't care. I hadn't seen them in a while; I hadn't even visited them in the hospital since I'd started college. Mostly, I needed something to take my mind off everything, but it was too early in the day to start partying.

My father's lab was in the basement, in a hard-to-find corner of the hospital that I'm sure conducted creepy experiments back in the olden days before HIPAA and moral regulations existed. Just to get there was a journey of elevators, stairs, and deserted hallways.

The descent always reminded me of what the hospital was like back in 2020, when only patients and doctors were allowed inside. It was so bare then, without family members, visitors, and a good portion of the staff. I was lucky to have Chase let in, and he had to stay quarantined in my room with me.

When I finally got to the lab, the door was closed. A beefy but bored security guard stood blocking the entrance.

That was strange.

The hospital's security team usually roamed around during their shifts or stood guarding important patients. I hadn't remembered seeing one at my dad's lab before. He researched stem cells. He didn't practice on celebrities or anything.

The guard straightened up as I approached. "You can't go in there."

"What?" I had been visiting my dad since I was a kid.

He huffed and repositioned himself to try and look more intimidating. "I said, you can't go in there."

"But this is my dad's lab."

"Look, kid, I don't care if you're the Queen of England, you can't—"

He was interrupted by voices ringing from up the hall. I could tell from their tone that their conversation was supposed to be hushed, but the hallway was so old and echoey that we could hear them clearly even before they came into sight.

"I'm just saying that now is the perfect time to shut down Pandora! The virus is under control, and most citizens are getting their regular booster shots to ensure that it can't flare up again! No one else has to get hurt," a voice whispered.

"'Perfect time'?" scoffed the other voice. "You've been saying this since the beginning. Besides, this has never just been about the virus, you know that. Even you can't predict the future, Sam. What if—"

And then, they rounded the corner.

"Well, hello there, kiddo!" Dr. Hunt's entire demeanor changed as he saw me standing at the end of the hall. "This is a wonderful surprise. Are you here to see your dad?"

"Trying to, Sam," I said with a weak laugh and gesture toward the guard. "Apparently you guys are VIPs now."

Dr. Samuel Hunt was my dad's best friend and had been his research partner for as long as I could remember. They were adorably dorky together and always gave each other bowties for Christmas. He smiled more than anyone else I knew. Hearing him so upset was strange, it and made me wonder what project he had been talking about.

"Sorry about that. Daniel can be a little, um, enthusiastic, but he's supposed to keep people out of our lab." The other man was, of course, my dad, Dr. Thomas Bell. He was a bit taller, with salt n' pepper hair and wild eyebrows that stuck up everywhere and drove my mom, Astrid Bell, absolutely crazy. "Why don't you go visit Astrid? We're actually kind of busy today, sweetie."

Sam chimed in. "Plus, your mom's office has a nicer coffee machine."

"Oh, okay." My disappointment must have read on my face, because my father frowned and pulled me in for a deep hug.

"I'm sorry, sweetie. Why don't we get dinner this weekend?"

I nodded. "Tomorrow? It will be nice to get a break from the food they serve here."

"The Wollstone dining hall not up to par with your favorite restaurants?" asked Sam.

I mimed vomiting and they both laughed, which seemed to annoy the security guard.

Good. He looked like he hadn't laughed in ages.

My mom's office was not tucked away in a corner of the hospital. It was on the top floor, next to the rest of top administrators, and looked new age with frosted glass walls and a beautiful view of the city. Just to make it to the door, I had to give my name and be buzzed in by two secretaries, Anna and Kim.

My parents were one of those "opposites attract" kind of couples. My dad was book-smart—well, book brilliant—and a bit of a nerd, but my mom was charming and charismatic.

My dad couldn't name a single Kardashian or half the people on our Christmas card mailing list, but my mom knew more names than the entire US Census. My dad's face was an open book, always giving away exactly what he was thinking. Everything about my mom, though, from her facial expressions and her word choices to when and where she interacted with someone, was all deliberate.

Today, mom was wearing a pantsuit that would have made Hilary Clinton jealous, with a pearl necklace that matched her teeth when she flashed me a brilliant smile.

"Ivy! This is a surprise!"

I walked over to the table where she kept her coffee machine and five different kinds of flavoring syrups and began to make myself a mocha. "I just saw Dr. Thana."

"Oh?" Mom's voice remained neutral. I always wondered how she felt when I brought up my mental health. I couldn't help remembering how broken she had seemed last summer when I woke up in the psych ward. My parents had both been on the verge of tears for weeks; it was unnerving.

"It was fine," I said and tried to change the conversation, just in case. (I couldn't deal with too many additional emotions today; I had already had enough.) "Afterward I went to visit Dad and…" I trailed off for a moment and finished stirring my coffee. "Why was there a guard there?"

My mother gestured for me to sit down in the chair across from her desk. "How was therapy? Do you still think it's working?"

Was she changing the subject because she knew I had changed it? Or was she avoiding the question? After all, like mother, like daughter. We used the same tactics.

"It was fine." I tried to change the subject again. "I got tickets to the Democracy Ball! It's in December, so I'll need to get a dress soon."

"I'll order some for you to try on. Do you still like Dr. Thana?"

Ugh. I should *not* have talked to my parents right after therapy. I should have waited until later, until I could separate myself from all the feelings I'd dragged up.

I had worried my parents enough for a lifetime. I didn't want to do it anymore.

"Yeah, Mom. She's great!" I tried to inject some sincerity into my tone. "You know what, I just remembered I need to return a book to the library, and if I do it after five o'clock there's an extra day's fine."

I had no idea if she bought that. I hadn't voluntarily gotten a book from the library since high school.

"But Dad said you guys would be up for dinner tomorrow!" I added quickly.

She looked at me for a moment, analyzing my face before she said, "That sounds great. I'll tell my secretary to make a reservation. I love you, Ivy."

Oops. I almost felt bad for lying.

"I love you too, Mom."

But it was for the best.

CHAPTER FOUR

IF KIDS THESE DAYS WOULD LOOK UP FROM THEIR DAMN CELL PHONES, I WOULD NOT HAVE BEEN AMBUSHED BEHIND A TREE

My thoughts were whirling as I left the hospital and started to walk back to my room in Witt Hall. The day had already been long, and it was only about six o'clock. *Thank God for the weekend.* I desperately needed to unwind and have some fun.

Outside was beautiful. The storm had cleared out, leaving only the cool blue autumn sky hanging above. Maple trees lined the path, occasionally dripping rainwater. Witt Hall stood in the distance, brick and old-fashioned, with the vines of my namesake slowly creeping up the walls.

It seemed so peaceful outside of my head, so calm and orderly. I tried to imagine what my life would be like if I had never been depressed or had anxiety. Who would I have been?

A buzz from my phone interrupted my thoughts: a text from Emilia in our group-chat. *"Y'all, I heard that Eli is gonna be at the GCC party tonight!"*

Aiden's response came a moment later. "*Who?*"

"*Boy from club*," Will sent.

"*If Will sexiles me again tonight, can I come stay in 603?*" asked Harrison.

"*Ivy already invited a rat to live with us, what's an additional Southern boy or two?*" Emilia shot back.

I laughed aloud and quickened my pace a little, excited to get back to my friends and away from all my horrible memories at the hospital. In the crisp fall air, it was easy to forget last summer, to ignore strange dreams, to tell myself it didn't matter if there was something strange going on in the basement of this hospital. I had a party to look forward to, alcohol to drink, and friends who let me adopt a rat. The only condition had been that I buy him actual rat equipment to replace the cardboard box and that we name him Whiskers so we can call him Whiskey for short.

My life was perfect.

"*Uf—*"

I saw a blur of motion, but before I could turn to examine it, I was tackled from the side. I fell to the ground and found myself lying in grass being squeezed in a viselike grip by…

It couldn't be.

I squeezed my eyes shut.

But when I opened them again, he was there.

Chase Kennedy was here, on Wollstone campus. He was here, tangled with me in the grass, alternating between hugging and sobbing and squeezing my hands so tightly that I thought the bones would break. He was here.

Impossible.

Was this a dream? No, I never noticed impossible things in a dream, not while I was still in them. I always accepted the situation right until I woke up. Then what was this? How could Chase be standing there, crying, and murmuring my name over and over again like a prayer?

He looked worse, and I was pretty sure that wasn't just my imagination being spiteful. His eyes were ringed by enormous black bags, and his dark hair, usually so carefully arranged, was now long and messy. His clothes were loose and wrinkled. *Did he lose weight?* And then I noticed *what* he was wearing. Chase Kennedy, the boy who dressed like life was a business brunch and he was there to drink free mimosas, stood before me in baggy sweatpants tied in place with a piece of yarn and an overstretched T-shirt.

I had been a little disappointed when we first started dating that Chase wasn't the sort of boy I could steal an old sweatshirt from. I had seen girls do it on TV; the sweatshirts were always big and soft and held the boy's scent for when they were apart. I didn't stay disappointed for long, though. Within a month he had gifted me with the Chase version of old sweatshirt: his Ralph Lauren quarter zip and oversized Burberry sunglasses. The pieces smelled like him and everything, all smoke and bergamot, and I hadn't even had to ask.

He had just surprised me one day, showing up to our spot with the gift and a light pink rose. I'd been so deliriously happy that day. I wanted to give him something too, but all I had on me was a gym bag. Chase went home that day with a T-shirt from my school's girl's golf team that had the word "Bell" ironed on the back.

Oh. Chase wasn't wearing *a* stretched-out T-shirt. He was wearing *my* stretched-out T-shirt.

"Ivy," he was still saying, his voice broken up by the tears. "Ivy, it's you, oh my god, it's you. You're alive. I can't believe it, you're alive!"

I smelled his breath then. *Oh god. He's stopped regularly brushing his teeth.* These were symptoms of depression.

I pushed him off me. "What are you doing?" I looked around wildly but saw only the empty pathway, the grass, and the trees.

"You're still here!" he gasped, sounding louder than before. "You're still here, you're alive, oh my god, Ivy! I thought that was you. I mean, I got to campus last Monday, and I thought I saw you, but you were with all your friends, and so I was waiting for you to be alone, and I didn't want to get my hopes up, but I kept looking. I saw you coming out of the hospital and... Ivy, I just can't believe you're alive!"

I was shaking. "I'm... alive? You thought I might not be?" My words, which were supposed to sound cold, came out broken instead.

I felt something warm trickling down my arm. I looked down and saw a thin line of red blood oozing down my forearm. I must have scraped it when I fell.

"You thought I would be dead, Chase? Three months later?" I asked slowly, still trying to process what was happening, waiting for it to suddenly make sense. "You thought that if you dumped my ass, after I tried to kill myself, I would be so depressed I wouldn't be alive to face you three months later?"

His face was frozen now, his expression locked in horror. His angular features were twisted so badly it seemed to be causing him actual pain.

"Wait, what are you talking about, Ivy? What are you saying? I don't—"

I interrupted him. I let the words I had been avoiding to think for months roll off my tongue. I let my pain turn into anger.

"Where the *fuck* do you get the nerve, Chase Kennedy? You waltz out of my life months ago, with a *text message* about how I'm *not worth it*? You ignore me for months! And then you think you can just waltz back in, push me behind a tree, and act all pleasantly surprised that I'm alive?"

He was stammering now and put his hands on my shoulders. "I don't... I don't understand. I mean, I don't know what you're—"

I tried to pull away, but he wouldn't let me. Now, I really was mad.

"No," he said. "I don't... I—"

"Should I refresh your memory?" I grabbed my phone, which had fallen when he tackled me.

"But, Ivy," he said, "I don't get what you're saying. I didn't know you were here. I didn't leave, I just—"

I pushed my phone in his face, the screen now showing the last text he had sent me, the conversation marked "Chase Kennedy <3" because I hadn't been able to look at it for long enough to delete the heart from his contact.

"'I'm sorry,'" he read aloud, his voice shaky. "'But you're just not worth it anymore.'"

That sentence didn't sound how I imagined it when I read the text this summer. In my head his voice was tired, exhausted after dealing with me and my two near-death incidents. It sounded dejected, like he was a little sad about it but had already begun to detach, like when you finish an interesting show on Netflix but already have a couple more lined up to start next.

That sentence was not supposed to sound like this, so shattered and... hiccup-y. It wasn't supposed to sound like this at all, and yet, hearing those words read aloud in the voice I had been thinking about for months, I couldn't help but begin to cry too.

In our three years together, I had only seen Chase this emotional once: in 2020, when I was sick. The rest of the time he was smirking, sarcastic, and confident if a bit rude. On his worst days he could be an asshole, but he had never been this—never broken.

Was this an act? Some kind of manipulation?

"Oh, Ivy," he said. He reached his hand out, as though he was about to wipe my tears, but hesitated. "Can you... I mean, would you please, please tell me everything you remember? What happened to you?"

I shook my head in disbelief. "I *remember*," I spat between tears, "dating you for three years. I *remember* you being there for me, for three years, even when I got coronavirus. I *remember* you saying I was worth it, calling me princess, saying you loved me, right up until it stopped being convenient for you. I *remember* you walking away instead of dropping me at the hospital or even calling nine-one-one when I wanted to die. And I *remember*," I sobbed, "waking up alone in a hospital bed, waking up hating you with every fiber of my being, waking up and all that was left of you was that stupid text."

Chase didn't say anything. He looked as though all the life had been drained from him, and if we hadn't been on the ground already I would have worried he was going to collapse.

"If you needed to leave," I said, my voice getting quieter as my anger grew, "you could have done it. We were about to go to college, and I know mental health problems can be a lot to take on. You could have told me you needed some space, and I would have understood. At least, I *think* I would have. But you didn't. You were a coward; you abandoned me, and you did it in the douchiest way possible."

"Ivy, I never wanted to hurt you." His plea sounded genuine, but I wasn't falling for it. "I didn't realize, I mean... Oh God, Ivy. I need a minute to think. I'm so sorry, but can you please just give me a minute to figure out what to do here? I'm not sure what I can tell you. I'm not sure how you'll react. I just need a minute."

How could he not realize how selfish he sounded?

"Take a minute," I growled. "Take a thousand minutes! Take them all. In fact, why don't you take forever, and why don't the two of us never talk again?"

And then, I did the only thing I could think to do. I pushed myself off the grass and ran.

***

"*Viva la Rome!*" yelled Emilia.

Five glasses clinked together, then tipped back.

"Disgusting," said Aiden, barely audible over the sound of Britney Spears's "Toxic." "Where did we buy this vodka?"

I rolled my eyes. "Sarah from debate bought it for us, and it actually tastes fantastic when you consider the fact that it was twelve dollars for the whole handle."

"This was twelve dollars?"

"Yep!"

Aiden shrugged. "Cheers then." He smiled, and we tapped our empty glasses together.

"You'll never guess what I learned today," Emilia said, bringing the bottle around to top us off. "That girl you liked? Her name is Henley Gara. She's a freshman too, *and* she just got elected to the board of the GCC."

I choked on a mouthful of vodka. "As a freshman?"

"Apparently one of the board members just got expelled because they found out he bribed his way into Wollstone, so they held a special election to find a replacement."

Oh my god. As if I needed another reason to avoid Henley. Most of the board members were power hungry, the kind who would run for Congress someday just because they could. Not the kind of people to whom you wanted to bare your heart and soul. My instincts must have been off when I felt that pull to her in the square. *Have my instincts ever been* on?

I set down my glass and walked over to my vanity to finish my makeup for the night.

"Getting ready for your hot date?" asked Will.

I scrunched my nose up in mock annoyance. "*Et tu*, Will? It's not a date! We've never actually talked, and I was planning to go to the GCC party before I even knew she was on the board."

"If it's not a date," asked Emilia with a smirk, "then why are you putting on your good lipstick?"

I froze, the pink tube still in my hand. "That doesn't mean anything! I just want to be able to polish off a few more shots tonight, and this is the only lipstick that won't rub off when I drink."

I'd been working on my look for the past two hours, ever since I had escaped Chase. I had needed a distraction, a way to get him off my mind, and what better way than to dress the fuck up and have meaningless sex with a stranger?

I was wrapped in a white sheet as my toga, which was secured in place with a little clear tape and a pretty gold belt. I was wearing chunky gold bracelets, gold earrings, and a small golden crown I had borrowed from a friend. My eyeliner was winged, accentuating the glittering eye shadow I had spent twenty minutes applying, and my blonde hair hung loose in big curls. I looked awesome.

In the reflection, I caught a glimpse of Whiskey chugging along on the little pink exercise wheel that had just arrived from Amazon this morning. "Someone give Whiskey a treat or something," I called as I added one last dab of highlight on the tip of my nose. "It's the weekend for him too."

Will laughed and went to the fridge to pull out a couple grapes off the bunch we had stolen from the dining hall. I smiled when I heard Whiskey squeak a little in excitement and turned to watch as he hopped off the wheel and went to get his snack.

"Where's your hot date tonight, Harrison?" inquired Emilia.

"Rose is going out clubbing in Dupont with her business friends tonight," he responded. "Which means I will be acting as your wingman for the evening."

"Thank God," said Aiden, who was filling all our glasses with another round. "You're so much better at it than the girls."

Emilia and I both looked at him with exaggerated expressions of offense.

"What?" he asked, passing the drinks out. "Bi women are the worst wingmen. By the time you get someone over to one of us they've already decided they want to sleep with *you*!"

I threw a hand over my mouth and gaped in mock horror. "Am I hearing a little misogyny there, Aiden? Will's bi too."

"Do you *hate* women?" Emilia joined in. "Aiden Ricci, your mother would be ashamed of you."

He raised his eyes to the ceiling dramatically, "Just because I don't understand women on any level doesn't mean I'm not a feminist. I don't mind Will because we're both governed by the same bro code. I understand what the rules are. With you two, though, I have no fucking clue how it's supposed to work."

Will nodded his agreement. "See, he's not being sexist, he's being *homophobic*. Much better."

Aiden snorted, shutting his eyes for a moment, and his mouth curved into a smile.

"Okay," Em declared. "One more toast before we leave. Do we know any other Latin phrases to toast with?"

"*Carpe Diem*?" Harrison suggested helpfully at the same time I offered, "*Eers-chay*?"

"*Habeas Corpus!*" added Will.

I crinkled my eyebrows. "The arrest thing?"

"It's more like the right to a judge, I think. It's supposed to protect you from unlawful imprisonment."

"Oh." *Why were the most random things in Latin?*

"I'm on an article called 'Twenty-Seven Latin Phrases That Haven't Died Out Yet,'" said Aidan, looking intently at his phone. "I'm looking for a good party phrase."

We all huddled around him, reading over his shoulder as he scrolled.

"Wait! What about that one?" asked Em, and Aiden's finger froze in place. "'They have lived.' That sounds good, right?"

"I like it!" Harrison grinned. "Like 'yolo,' but instead of being outdated by ten years, it's outdated by two thousand."

Will and I nodded our agreement, and we raised our final toast. "*Vixere!*" we cheered.

It wasn't until ten minutes later that I noticed Aiden frowning at his phone as the five of us walked together to the party.

I sped my pace up for a second to fall in step with him and linked my arm through his. "What's up?" I asked. "Is everything okay?"

Aiden nodded slowly, but the frown didn't leave his face. "It's fine, it doesn't actually matter. I was just looking up that word we used for the toast. I wanted to see what the Romans used it for."

"And?" I prompted, trying not to laugh at how in character that was. We were going to a party on a Friday, and Aiden was double checking the proper Latin translation of a toast.

"*And*," he said, "it does technically translate to 'they have lived,' but it was kind of famously used for something else."

"Not a toast?"

"An execution."

"Oh."

We leaned in closer to each other as a shard of icy wind blew past, tossing our loose strands of toga back and forth. I could hear the faint roar of the party in the distance, growing louder with each step we walked.

"'They have lived?'" I asked, to break the silence.

"'They *have* lived. Past tense."

"Oh." I realized what he was getting at. "They already died?"

"Yeah. Kind of a morbid way to toast a party," he said, laughing a little.

I stayed silent a beat too long.

"You know it doesn't actually matter, right?" He looked down at me, eyes narrowing a little in focus. "It's just a dumb mistake. Don't get superstitious on me now, Bell."

I flashed him a wry smile. "I'm *incredibly*-stitious," I joked. "Why do you think I spend so much time trying to befriend the Wollstone ghosts?"

Aiden chuckled. The rest of our friends fell into step with us, and the conversation changed course.

I smothered the uneasy thoughts racing around my head, forcing myself to replace security guards and stalker ex-boyfriends with thoughts of the weekend ahead of us.

Still, I couldn't help thinking to myself, *we should have just gone with "eers-chay."*

CHAPTER FIVE

IF I HAD REMEMBERED TO EAT DINNER, CHASE WOULD STILL HAVE HIS SHOES

—

By the time we got to the party, the Hamilton rooftop was already packed. Hamilton was an upperclassmen dorm, decorated with huge balconies that made it a prime party locale. It took six flights of stairs just to get to the top—which was not an easy feat for anyone both tipsy and in heels—but god was it worth it.

"I'll go get us some drinks," yelled Aiden over the noise, and I nodded as I pushed my way over to the edge of the roof.

Even with the three extra inches from my stilettos, I was still far shorter than most of the crowd. It might have been easiest to let Will go first, tall as he was, but I figured that God gave me pointy elbows for a reason, so I may as well use them. Wollstone was one of those small schools where everyone seems to know each other, and I was enough of an extrovert that I was on a first name basis with nearly half the crowd. But I kept my head down and my elbows out. I wasn't in the mood to make eye contact with anyone.

I made my way, slowly but surely, to the edge of the roof, like a river eroding a canyon in the earth. The view of the Potomac was dazzling, even after all this time. I had always thought I might get used to it, the same way I had gotten used to clubbing with royalty and studying politics with future presidents, but I never could. It was simply too fantastic to be familiar.

Across the water, the city lights of Deloitte and McKinsey glimmered: the modern-day palaces Wollstone's students fought to invade after graduation. To the left stood the monuments, displayed proudly like jewels in a crown. The stars covered it all, glittering like diamond dust scattered across the pitch-black sky.

And when, after years of soaking in the beauty of it all, I turned back to the party, I saw students, smushed together, dancing, drinking, and kissing, framed beneath the soft glow emitting from the historic Gotland clock tower. Students, who would someday be scattered among the high-rises and the House, making the decisions that kept the world from crumbling, but for now were just living and smiling and having fun, like other young people anywhere else in the world.

I had tried, my first time here, to take pictures, to capture it all for the later years when my memories might fail. It didn't work, though. Nothing could truly contain it all, this fantasy world that existed at my fingertips. I had to enjoy it now—to embrace this place with the knowledge that it was entirely temporary—though in four years it would belong to an entirely different girl.

And I had to be okay with that.

"All they had was jungle juice, and not the good kind."

I turned to see Emilia, Aiden, and Harrison coming toward me holding red solo cups.

"My taste buds might be permanently damaged after this," said Aiden. He swirled his cup and wafted the scent toward himself like we were at a wine tasting. "I'm getting notes of… rat poison, the solution from the bottom of an empty Lysol Wipes, and Absinthe, 2023—a great year for it."

Harrison laughed. "Mine has a bunch of Skittles at the bottom. It looks like they're all melding together into one giant Super Skittle." He passed me a cup, and I took a long drink.

"Oh! Mine has gummy bears!" I said as I grimaced at the lingering burn. "Where's Will?"

Aiden pointed across the party. I followed this gaze to see two boys making out against a railing. One of them was Will, and the other one was…

"Is that…" I asked.

"Eli," Emilia said. "He met him the last time we went clubbing."

I heard a roar of cheers from the center of the crowd. I turned to look, but all I could see was two brown feet in strappy black sandals swaying upside down above the crowd.

"What's going on?" I asked Harrison, who towered at least ten inches above me.

He peered over the crowd. "Oh! Henley's doing a keg stand." He glanced down at me, "You could do it better though; she has people holding up her ankles."

"Who's the Roman god of keg stands?" I asked

"It doesn't matter," Em grinned. "The one you need tonight is Cupid."

Harrison scrunched his eyebrows together. "Is Cupid Roman? I thought he was Greek."

"That's Eros." Aiden eyed me. "But I think Ivy's patron would be Zeus."

I frowned. "The lightning guy?"

"The fuckboy."

"Ahh." I smiled. "Maybe. Okay, yeah, that sounds good." I drained the last of my cup and announced that I was going to look for refills.

For the next hour or so, I socialized, flirted, and drank. A lot. The night grew colder and the stars fuzzier. The music seemed to lose its lyrics bit by bit, until all I could hear was bass. At one point, I caught my reflection in my dark phone screen as I pulled it out to check a text and realized that I only had one earring on. Oh well.

Someone brought out a ping pong table for a game of beer pong, and I found myself on a team with four junior boys, two on either side of me, laughing hysterically as we tried and failed to aim our shots across the table. I didn't know *why* our inability to aim was so funny. It just was.

"Look at you, hogging all of the boys," came an amused voice in my ear.

I looked up to see a pretty girl in a light pink toga, wearing sparkly silver makeup. Her coiled black hair was wound up into two high buns.

"I certainly wasn't intending to," I grinned. "You're welcome to take my place…"

"Yona," she filled in.

"Ivy," I responded. "You know, I really was about to leave."

Yona and I were pressed together on the landing of a fire escape when we finally heard her friends calling her name.

After the second iteration, she sighed and yelled back, "I'm down here!"

Three faces peered down at us.

"Yon!"

Her friends were grinning, and I realized we were still holding each other. "Maybe we should..." I trailed off, and Yona sighed again before she nodded.

We parted, slowly, until only our hands were intertwined.

"We have to go!" her friend said.

"Add me on snap?" Yona asked and let go of my hand. "That was, you know, nice," she finished, one corner of her mouth turning up in a smile.

I nodded, smiling too. I pulled out my emergency eyeliner pen from the waistband pocket of my spandex and held out my forearm so she could write her username there.

Then, after one last, fleeting kiss, she was gone.

For a moment I stood on the landing, blinking a little and trying to orient myself. *Where was everyone? Oh! I had my phone!*

I pulled up my texts, squinting at the too-bright screen.

I saw three from Emilia, all sent over the course of two hours. The first mentioned that Will had left without mentioning the name of the boy with whom he had gone. The next two were from just twenty minutes ago.

"Aiden and Harr and I went home. You looked like you were... Busy :) :)."

"Let us know when you're ready to go home! One of us will come and walk you back. Love you, babe <3."

Oh. I thought briefly about the walk home through the frigid autumn air. I didn't totally want to do it alone, but if they were already at Witt, I didn't want to make them walk back just to get me, either. It was all the way on the other side of campus, and they were surely drunk and tired too.

I picked my way slowly up the stairs, back to the party, so I could look for someone I knew. The night was winding down: the roof was only half as full as it had been. I spotted the drinks table, still stocked with Natty Lite cans and jungle juice, and suddenly noticed how thirsty I felt. I pushed my way over to grab a cup.

"Ivy?" There was a boy standing by the table, popping open a can of beer. He had sandy hair and was a little shorter than average, but he looked muscular, like he could bench me and Emilia at the same time if he wanted. Was he a Wollstone athlete or something? His outfit seemed to point to that; he was wearing mesh athletic shorts and a Wollstone tank top. How did I know him?

Ugh. I hated my crappy memory. If Will had been here, he could have told me the boy's name, zodiac sign, and exactly how I knew him. *You two sat next to each other on the second day of orientation. He was the guy who gave us free season tickets after we met him at a soccer team party.*

"Hey, you!" I said, making my voice extra bright to try to cover the awkward pause. "How are you?" I took a swift sip from my cup.

The boy smiled, not seeming to notice anything was off. "Honestly, I'm exhausted. I was just about to head out. You?"

Thank God.

"Me too!" I chugged the rest of the drink and threw it in the trash. "Want to walk together?"

He beamed. "Yeah, I would love some company! You're in Witt, right?"

I nodded, trying not to show how relieved I was. I didn't want to seem desperate, but knowing that I wouldn't have to walk back alone was *amazing*.

We picked our way down the stairs, the boy holding me gently by the waist when I stumbled. I was just grateful I wouldn't have to wake up tomorrow with "I fell down three flights of stairs" bruises to explain at dinner with my parents.

When we were finally back at ground level, he moved his grip from my waist to my hand, and I let him lead the way. The stars were beautiful, even if my eyes weren't entirely able to bring them into focus.

God, I was so lucky to live in DC. And I was so, so lucky to have such good friends. And I was so, so, so—

The deafening wail of a car horn cut off my train of thought. I shrieked as the boy pulled me out of harm's way, my breath suddenly fast and shallow.

"Oh my god!" I gasped. "I could have..." I blinked. Adrenaline coursed through my body, and I focused my surroundings for the first time since we left the party. The car's taillights were fading away, driving past townhouses.

Where were the dorms?

"Umm, where are we?" I asked, trying not to panic. "What are you doing?"

The boy didn't bother to glance down at me.

"Small detour. I just need to drop something off at my car." He kept walking, still holding my hand, but I didn't move.

"Your car?" Wollstone students didn't have cars. Parking in the District was horrible; the university didn't even let seniors have them.

"Wait," I said, my brain feeling very slow.

Something else was wrong.

I thought about when he'd first said hello to me, when I'd try to remember how I knew him. I hadn't come up with anything, I'd only guessed that he was on a team because of his outfi—

"Why aren't you wearing a toga?"

"What?" He finally stopped.

"We were at a toga party. Everyone else was wearing one. Why aren't you?"

I saw his eyes dart down to my own toga, just for a second, before they were back on my face. "I came from another party; I didn't have time to change."

That kind of made sense. Right? Maybe I was overthinking it. I mean, I did have a lot to drink, too. But still....

"Come on, I need to get home soon," he said, and this time he pulled so hard that I stumbled, nearly tripping. I only stayed upright because of the tightness of his grip.

Did he suddenly have an accent? No, that wouldn't make sense. He's probably too drunk and slurring his words.

"Hey!" I heard a familiar yell, "Let her go!"

I was really losing it.

The boy swore under his breath—again, the accent, he was chewing on the vowels—and then he let me go.

My world turned horizontal. I felt the coolness of the pavement beneath my face before I felt the pain of my head smacking against it.

In the distance I could see the boy getting smaller as he sprinted away.

And then Chase's face was close to mine. He was asking me if I was okay.

"Of course I am," I tried to tell him, but even I knew that I was slurring the words.

"Should I take you to the hospital?"

"No hospital!"

"Okay," he agreed.

Chase pulled me upright and let me lean on him for support as the world threatened to tip sideways again. "Who was that guy?"

I searched my foggy memories, but I still couldn't remember his name or if I had ever seen him before. "No idea. I thought he was a student, but then he wasn't." Suddenly the situation seemed absurd, and I was laughing. "I have *no idea* who that was! That's *weird*, right?"

My laughter grew frantic. I didn't care.

"Why are you here?" I asked Chase. I knew I probably sounded rude, considering that he had just saved me, but adrenaline and alcohol had stolen my filter. "Are you stalking me?"

"A little," he admitted. "I was worried about you, and I didn't know what else to do. I'm so confused, about what happened, what you remember, and then I saw that guy and you were struggling, and I panicked."

"I'm still mad."

My head felt heavy. I let it sink into his chest. *God, this was comfortable.* So familiar, like his body was memory foam that had been holding my place just in case.

"I know you're still mad, Ivy," Chase sighed. "I promise I'm trying to figure this out."

He was quiet for a moment.

"What did they do to you?" he whispered, so softly I wasn't sure if he really wanted an answer.

I looked up at Chase. I examined his face, his earnest eyes dark as the sky above us and even more beautiful. I could tell, in that moment, that he really didn't want to hurt me.

I almost believed that he hadn't wanted to hurt me last summer.

For that one, strange moment, everything was normal. I smiled.

And then I vomited all over his expensive shoes.

CHAPTER SIX

IF I HADN'T HAD THOSE EXTRA ESPRESSO SHOTS, I WOULDN'T HAVE MADE IT THROUGH THE DAY

———

The first thing I noticed was the cold. My fingers were stiff, and every breath felt like a million tiny knives.

There was a flash, and then everything was bathed in a bright fluorescence. Why was it so bright? It was far, far too bright, like staring into the sun. It *hurt*.

I was in a lab, a medical research lab like my dad's. It was familiar… almost. There were things I recognized: petri dishes and hypodermic needles and Xray machines. There were other things, though, things that even I hadn't seen after a lifetime of two parents working in a hospital. Mirrors lined every possible surface. A piece of equipment like a big dryer you might find at a hair salon was there, except on closer inspection it was lined with speakers instead of vents.

I shuffled forward, still so cold. There was a fish tank, but it was huge, the size of a car, and when I stuck my hand inside I realized it wasn't filled with water but a clear, slimy gel.

What was this place? I turned again and saw a countertop filled with charts and papers. It was all handwritten, even the intricate tables filled with hundreds of lines of data, and something was strange about it. I stared at the writing for ages before I realized with a start that... it was my own.

"You won't find what you're looking for, princess. Not over there."

I spun around and saw Chase standing across from me on the other side of the lab. He was wearing a blue button-up and khakis, like he was on his way to a boat party and just happened to stop by this creepy lab. He looked smug with one eyebrow raised; the haughty expression looked foreign on his normally sweet face. Next to him was a metal table covered in a white sheet. Except... was someone under that sheet? Were we alone in here?

"You won't find what you're looking for," Chase repeated, and I looked down at the paper I was holding. Written on it was a single word, scrawled a hundred times in angry red ink.

Pandora.

I dropped the paper and began walking slowly toward Chase. "What am I looking for?" I asked him. "Do you know?"

"I know what you think you're looking for," he said, smirking. "But I also know you're not ready to find it."

I moved closer, desperate. "Is it Pandora? Who is she?"

He laughed. "See, I told you. You're not ready."

"Shut up!" I cried. "Shut up, shut up, shut up!" Why was he laughing like that? Chase, *my Chase*, could never make a sound so cruel.

I pushed past him, over to the metal table.

***

The first thing I noticed was the heat. I was in my bed, in room 603, covered in fluffy pink blankets, and the room was bright with sunlight. It wasn't cold. There was no lab, no body. Of course there was no body, *obviously* there was no body. *It was just a dream.*

I slowed my breathing. I focused on my bed, my room. This was real. My sparkly pillows with cliché feminist quotes were real. The giant fish tank filled with slime was not real. Whiskey, curled up in his tiny bed, was real. *The body on a metal table was not real.* I knew that.

So why did I keep having these dreams?

"Thank God you're finally awake. I'm starving."

I looked over and saw Will, Aiden, and Harrison piled together on Emilia's lilac comforter. Will pulled off the emerald green Wollstone sweatshirt that he was wearing over a long-sleeved tee and tossed it over to me. "Put this on. We're going to Company."

I pulled myself reluctantly out of bed, nearly toppling over the edge before I managed to stand up.

Glancing down, I saw that my toga had unraveled at some point in the night, and I was left wearing just a bra and tight black spandex. Probably not the right look for brunch. I threw on the sweatshirt and grabbed my oversized dark sunglasses before walking to my vanity to put my hair in a ponytail.

In the mirror, my face looked even more exhausted than I felt, with dark mascara making me look more like a raccoon than a human and a scrape running along the left side of my face. Why hadn't I taken off my makeup when I got home last night? Or put on pajamas?

Come to think of it, how exactly had I gotten home? That part of the night was a little foggy.

Was there… vomit in my hair? *Ew.*

Before I could think about it for too long, Aiden coughed impatiently.

"All right, all right!" I said and grabbed my wallet. "Let's go."

Company was one of the most exclusive organizations on campus and kept up with the timeworn Wollstone tradition of nepotism and exclusivity. If you wanted to work for them, you had to know someone or be related to someone. Current members ran Wollstone's student grocery stores and coffee shops; alumni ran Fortune 500 companies. I hated the concept a little, but God damnit was their coffee good. Maybe privilege and disdain worked as secret ingredients.

As luck would have it, Company's cutest café was in the basement of our building, which was great, because I don't think I could have convinced my friends to walk the seven flights of stairs otherwise. We were all exhausted and hungover, but I was still a little scared of going in the elevator.

When we got there, Harrison and I grabbed our favorite booth while the rest of the group went to order our usuals. No hangover cure could top a chocolate chip scone and an iced mocha.

While we waited for our friends, I melted into the cozy booth. I was forever grateful that Company was designed for, and by, exhausted college students. It was exactly what I needed. The shop had soft seating, plenty of throw pillows, and lighting that was easy on the eyes. The walls were a gentle pastel color, and dreamy elevator music drifted throughout the room.

Weekend mornings were my favorite times at Wollstone, second only to weekend nights. During the nights, my friends and I would disperse throughout the campus as we hit the best parties, drank the best cocktails, and had the best time. In the mornings, we would assemble all the pieces we could remember into one fabulous, five-person story.

"Where are the rest of you?"

I looked up to see a wiry boy I recognized from our floor, standing paused near our table with one hand balancing a stack of pastries on a tray.

"Huh?" I asked, too tired to find a polite way to ask him to rephrase the question. *It's his fault, really. It should be common sense not to be cryptic before noon.*

"Your group?" He cocked his head at me and Harrison, and the pastries wobbled precariously. "It's never just one or two of you; you're like a matched set of five."

"Oh, right."

The boy walked away, leaving me to wonder why anyone would want to walk around alone.

"I got you a large," said Will when he returned with our pastries and drinks. He put my iced mocha in front of me with a smirk. "With *two* extra shots of espresso. You look like you need it."

"Especially if you're going to write that philosophy paper today," said Aiden, scooting into the booth next to me. "I still can't believe Whitby's giving you extra credit."

"Bimbo rights?" Em asked.

"I'm not a bimbo," I snapped, and I felt suddenly angry in a way that didn't match the playful tone my roommate had used.

Will raised one eyebrow skeptically. "You're hot, blonde, and dumb," he said, ticking off the words using three fingers on his left hand. He held his hand up like it was a court affidavit, case closed. "*Bimbo.*"

"I'm not dumb," I protested, but my voice was a bit quieter than it had been before.

"You know they're kidding, right?" asked Harrison, his brown eyes growing wide in concern. "You're, like, the opposite of a bimbo."

"A himbo?" Aiden asked.

"A smart girl!" Harrison insisted.

"Thanks, Harrison," I said. "I know they're kidding. I'm just tired." I sighed. "This philosophy paper is going to suck, and I need a power nap before I get dinner with my parents tonight."

"Wait!" cried Emilia, just a little too loudly. The students at the tables next over were clearly fighting their own hangover headaches; they glared frostily at my roommate. "Did you forget about the soccer game?" she added in a normal volume. "You know we're playing the Naval Academy today, right?"

I bit my lip, thinking it over. "I shouldn't. Philosophy is, like, my worst grade right now." If I failed that class, my parents would give me that *we're-not-mad-we're-disappointed* look and would probably tell me I should drop an extracurricular or part of my social life or something. I would rather drop *out*.

"Oof," said Will. "What time? Are you still going out with us tonight?"

I opened my mouth to tell him that *of course* I was going out, it was Saturday for God's sake, but paused when a whiff of hair-vomit reached my nose. *Gross.* I could stay in and go to bed early, or get ahead on Russian homework, or try to Facetime one of my old high school friends.

If I go to bed early, I'll just be falling that much sooner into the dreams. If I work on Russian, I'll have to confront how unbelievably horrible I am at it. If I Facetime someone from high school, they might ask what happened with Chase.

Best not.

"I'll be there," I said.

"Good!" Emilia took a bite of her croissant. "You'll never guess what happened last night."

Over the next hour, my friends and I unpacked the previous night. Apparently, Will and had gone home with Eli and woken up there at five in the morning. Meanwhile, Aiden and Emilia had accidentally hooked up with the same girl and only discovered it when they ran into her later as she was trying to flirt with Harrison.

Poor Harrison, ever the Southern gentleman, hadn't even realized she was doing it. The whole campus knew he and Rose were together, and most people left them alone. Rose, for her part, had texted Harrison that she had seen two professors making out on the dance floor of the club she was at. Two *married* professors—like, married to other people.

Surprisingly, however, the most interesting piece of gossip I heard had nothing to do with fighting, cheating, or sex: it was about the elevator. Aiden had heard, from a couple of his friends who had student jobs with Wollstone security, that last night the police were called into our dorm to rescue a group of freshmen. They had gotten too overly drunk at their pregame and hadn't even made it out of the building when they decided it would be funny to start jumping around in the elevator as it carried them down.

According to the police, the elevator was so old and finicky that two or more students were heavy enough to make it start or stop simply by jumping at the same time. So, the group last night had accidentally stopped the elevator when they jumped and hadn't realized they could make it start again.

I wasn't quite sure why I found this piece of information so interesting. It was just another story, one of many, but for some reason I kept turning it over and over in my head while my friends laughed on. It wasn't as though jumping in the elevator could have helped me. I had been alone when the elevator got stuck. I wouldn't have been heavy enough to shake it loose, even if I was brave enough to try. Why did the information seem important?

"Ivy?"

I looked up, dazed, to find four expectant faces looking back at me.

"It's your turn!" said Emilia. "Tell us about what happened last night!"

"Oh, right." I took a big sip of my mocha, trying to force my brain to wake up. "I made out with this girl, Yona. She was *so* beautiful and sweet. And then I came home!"

My friends looked confused.

"What?"

Aiden squinted at me, examining my expression. "Ivy," he said, "You didn't get home until two in the morning."

I shook my head. "That can't be right. I checked my phone before I left the party. I saw your texts…" I remembered getting to the party and seeing Henley. I remembered talking to Yona and kissing her on a fire escape.

I was sure of my night, up until the point that I checked my phone on the way out of the party. And then…

"Maybe I just got caught up in a conversation in the Witt lobby or something?" I tried.

Em frowned at me. "You were definitely on the other side of campus. You know your phone has location tracking turned on, right? We checked on you a couple times. You weren't here."

I took another sip of mocha and tried to think. It was as though the memories I needed were there, in my mind, but they sat across a lake that had just frozen over. I could see them from a distance, could even try to get to them, but the farther I strayed from shore the thinner the ice got and the more cracks began to form.

I checked my phone and saw that my friends had gone home. *Sand.* I carefully picked my way down the stairs, away from the party. *Ice.* I ran into... someone... *Crack.* I had the vaguest recollection of a boy I didn't know; he was being creepy... *Crack! Crack! Crack!* Chase.

I had run into Chase. Or had I?

I knew with an absolute certainty that he had been in my dream. That crazy laboratory had felt so real. I shivered. Had my brain made up Chase at the party as well? My hangover seemed to intensify.

"Okay," said Aiden, throwing me a life preserver. "We're not going to get anywhere right now, so how about we go to the game so you guys can flirt with soccer players? Maybe that will jog your memory."

I flashed him a grateful grin as my friends laughed. "Sounds perfect." I didn't know why I couldn't tell my friends about Chase. I didn't think they would judge me if he turned out to be a figment of my imagination, but they might worry about me, and that was far worse. I didn't want to burden them, but there was no explanation that was okay. Either I was going insane, or my ex was back.

I looked down at my forearm, almost afraid at what I might or might not see, but it was there. Plain as day. My arm had been scraped by a tree. I had really seen Chase yesterday, had really yelled at him outside the hospital. I hadn't dreamt it all, but I didn't know if that made me feel better or worse.

We gathered our things from the booth, and I hung back a moment to chug the last of my coffee. I had consumed so much caffeine I could practically feel it running through my veins as I combed through the last twelve hours, wondering how I could have had both such realistic dreams and bleary memories.

"Ivy?" asked Aiden.

"Coming!" I shoved my worries to the back of my mind. I had other, better things to think about, like soccer boys, surviving a family dinner, and another night of partying.

***

Even if my parents hadn't chosen a fancy restaurant for our dinner, they still might have disowned me if I showed up in the outfit I had picked to wear out later in the night. It was tight, sequined, and so small that I could fold it up and slide it into the pocket of my coat.

I showed up at La République in black pants and a nice blouse with the dress hidden in my pocket and my stilettos hidden in my bag. What my parents didn't know wouldn't hurt them.

"You look nice!" said my dad, grinning from ear to ear and raising his voice over the buzz of conversation.

The entryway was packed, mostly with tourists who were hoping to get a last-minute reservation. La République was one of those places where you might accidentally run into a member of the cabinet, and people seemed to like that. I liked their bread basket.

"Right this way, Ms. Bell, Doctor," said a hostess over the din. She grabbed three menus and led us to our table, away from the throngs of people. The restaurant itself was calm, lit by a dozen small chandeliers and full of live plants and greenery. In the middle of every table were flowers, and from every wall snaked cords of leaves and fairy lights.

"We haven't been here in a while," remarked my mother as she sat down. She was wearing a dark dress, and her brown hair looked nearly black in the dim light. She smiled at me, then picked up a menu. "Come to think of it, we haven't done anything in a while since you started college. You'll have to catch us up!"

Right. I had been preparing for this. Talking to my parents hadn't always confused me so much, but during high school it started to change. I wasn't a kid anymore, but I couldn't just jump into an adult relationship with them. I was independent, but they had still raised me. I was never quite sure what to say.

Some things were clearly off limits. I couldn't tell them anything about my sex life. Probably nothing about breaking school rules, like a pet rat. I shouldn't tell them how much I had been drinking, or how often I had gone out. But my classes had to be safe to talk about, right?

"Well, I'm taking a philosophy class! This weekend I'm writing an extra credit paper!" Our waiter came by with a list of specials and a basket of bread, so I grabbed a piece of pain aux noix.

"That's wonderful!" said my dad, taking a piece too. "What about?"

"Why I'm learning about philosophy." I began to spread butter.

"Why *are* you learning philosophy?" asked Mom.

Fuck. I took a big bite to stall and glanced around the restaurant to see if I could telepathically summon the waiter.

"Umm, because I have a passion for knowledge," I mumbled through a mouthful of bread.

Mom narrowed her eyes. "What's your grade now? Before the extra credit?"

Shit. "Why was there a guard outside Dad's lab?" The question made her change the subject yesterday, so maybe it would work now.

My parents exchanged a glance. Why were they being so shifty? I was the teenager here. I was supposed to be the one hiding stuff from my parents, not the other way around. And I haven't even brought up how weird Dad acted when I interrupted him and Sam. Now that I thought about it, it was weird that they had been arguing at all.

But when my mom answered, her tone was even, almost rational. "His project is being backed by a big investor, and they just wanted to add an extra layer of security to protect their assets."

"It makes me feel like a celebrity!" joked Dad.

"Oh!" Mom interjected. "Speaking of celebrities, did you hear they're filming a *West Wing* reunion near campus? Ivy, do you still have a crush on Rob Lowe?"

Maybe my depression and anxiety were getting worse and I was reading into this too much. That was one of the problems that came with my sucky mental health: I let my thoughts spiral a disgusting amount. Maybe my parents thought everything was fine but just didn't want to talk about work.

And maybe my ex-boyfriend wasn't really stalking me.

But I had to try. "Have you guys talked to the Kennedy's recently? Or heard anything about Chase?" My voice quivered at his name, and I felt a pounding in my brain.

There. Had they made eye contact, just for a second?

"Of course we haven't," responded my mom, her tone casual. *Too casual?* "Don't you remember? Mr. Kennedy was transferred to London for work. Not to mention, you and Chase have graduated high school and, well, moved on. Why would we talk to them?"

"No reason," I said quickly. "I just... I heard a rumor that he might be in town. That's all." Did they know why he was back?

"Chase?" My dad's bushy eyebrows knit together. His poker face was much worse than my mom's.

I was about to say something else, but the waiter came back to take our orders, and when he left my mom immediately started talking about a new ball gown she had ordered for me. Chase slipped my mind, replaced by thoughts of shiny green silk, and I didn't think about him for the rest of dinner.

Or at least, that's what I told myself.

CHAPTER SEVEN

IF DORM ROOMS HAD BALCONIES, I COULD HAVE AVOIDED HIM

———

The apartment was crowded with pulsing music and colorful lights. The five of us stood in the entryway with Will and Emilia at the front, scoping out the scene.

"There," said Em, with a pointed look toward the left side of the room.

I followed her gaze and saw Yona standing in the corner with a group of friends. She was the reason we were at this party. There were three more we had planned to attend this evening, but when I got home from dinner with my parents, my friends had told me they'd texted her and found she would be here tonight.

"Okay." I took a slow, deliberate breath. "I'll go talk to her, find out what happened, and then we can leave."

"Do you want one of us to come with you?" asked Harrison.

I shook my head. "I can do it."

I pushed slowly through the crowd. I wondered why I didn't feel more at ease. Usually, the waves of talking and dancing and laughter and *people* felt like home, like I belonged. Tonight, though, I felt separate, like I wasn't a part of the crowd. Maybe I was losing my mind.

"Hey!" Yona grinned as soon as she saw me. "Fancy seeing you here."

I forced myself to smile back. "Hey!" I chewed on the inside of my cheek. *Just ask.*

"Is everything okay?" Her eyes studied my face, growing concerned.

"Yeah, of course," I nodded. "I just have a totally random question: Do you remember what time we split up last night?"

"Umm…" She glanced over her shoulder at her friends, and I realized they had stopped their own conversations to watch us.

"Like, midnight," one of them said. "We had to run to a different party."

Midnight.

"Why? Is everything okay?" asked Yona again.

"Yes!" I tried to sound more convincing this time. "I just couldn't remember."

I needed to leave. I turned and started moving away quickly, pushing through the crowd. I hated this, I hated that I couldn't remember, I hated feeling like a screw up. I had done something stupid last night, and now my friends were trying to figure out what it was because they were responsible and put together and I was not. They remembered what they did, who they hooked up with. They didn't have random ex's chasing them down, and even if they did, they wouldn't let it mess with their heads like this. *Just me.*

"So?" Will asked when I reached them.

I plastered on a smile. "I was with Yona the whole night."

***

By the last party of the night, I was exhausted. I hadn't even had anything to drink, but I still felt awful. I was standing at the edge of the room, watching as my friends pulsed with the music and the vibrant crowd. Aidan and Will were sipping from cans of cheap beer, and Em was talking to a slender girl with white hair who stood at least a foot taller than her.

"Hey, you." The words came from within an inch of my right ear, producing an involuntarily shiver that rippled down my back and a tingling sensation at the base of my neck. "Normally, I hate hosting parties like this, but *damn*. Look at you." I heard a low whistle, still too close, and I wondered if my eardrum might rupture. *At least then I wouldn't have to hear to this bullshit.*

I turned toward the voice. *Ew.* The boy was dressed like he had just come from a golf course, with a backward baseball cap on his head. He looked like he had never cleaned a toilet in his entire life.

"My room is actually right back there," he said, gesturing toward a door at the edge of the apartment.

"I'm good," I said, trying not to sound too annoyed. The rest of my friends looked like they were happy here, and I didn't want to get us kicked out.

"Where are you from?" He stepped closer.

"Not here." I stepped back.

"What are you doing later?" He came forward again.

"Not this." I stepped backward and hit a wall. *Shit.*

"What's your name?"

"I—Anna."

"Anna! There you are, girl!" came an excited voice.

I turned to see who had said my fake name. *Oh my god. Henley.*

"I have been looking for you all night!" She playfully brushed my shoulder. "Let's go get a picture over there," she said. "Whoops!" She stumbled as she began leading me away from the now-scowling boy, and he let out a grunt of frustration.

Oh god. Hadn't I just been feeling pathetic for needing to be saved all the time? I could feel myself blushing; I probably looked like a tomato. *Fuck.*

"My name's actually not—" I tried to clarify.

"I know, Ivy." Henley laughed. "I was just trying to get you away from that guy. He was hitting on me earlier too. He's a total creep."

I stopped walking. "You know my name?"

"Yeah, you told me when we met three weeks ago." Henley frowned. "You don't remember it at all?"

"Of course I do," I lied. I wracked my brain for the memory, but nothing came up. *Maybe I should tell Dr. Thana about this.*

Henley studied my face. "I don't think you do. Well, that's interesting."

I grimaced. "I'm already embarrassed. You need to rub it in?" *After all the things I'd forgotten, I'd really had to forget her too?* At least that might explain why she had stood out to me in the square.

"What? Wait, no!" Her face contorted in an emotion I couldn't quite read. Panic, maybe? "No, I meant, umm... Well, it's embarrassing. For *me*. I had this great conversation with a pretty girl, and she didn't even remember me."

"I—" My mouth fell open. *Henley thinks I'm pretty?* "I forget things a lot. It's annoying, but..." I trailed off, trying to think of something clever to say. Usually, I was better at flirting. "But I wish I remembered you," I finished lamely.

Henley smiled. "It's not your fault. It's just a little strange to adjust to."

Say something. "You seem pretty memorable to me," I tried. "I mean, I saw you at that toga party, doing a keg stand for the GCC. How on earth did you make it on the board already?"

She raised her eyebrows playfully, so I was pretty sure she was joking when she responded, "Ambition and moral ambiguity."

I bit back a smile. "A powerful combination. What else has that gotten you?" I moved closer to her, just an inch.

"Lots of things," Henley grinned. "For instance, all the ladies love it."

"Yeah?" My head tilted, eyes flickered between her captivating round eyes and her perfect red lips.

"Absolutely." She stepped forward.

My heart felt fast, and my skin was burning, the way it does when you're warming up after being far too cold. I felt like my body was going into overdrive.

And then soft red lips met mine.

And every other sensation disappeared.

***

My mother sobbed as she stood next to the open casket lid. She was wearing a black satin dress, her face bare of makeup but covered in two layered masks. It was 2020, the year of the socially distanced funerals.

There were no hymnals in the church; you weren't allowed to sing at a 2020 funeral. Apparently, singing spread the particles through the air and put you at higher risk of spreading the virus.

You couldn't cry onto peoples' shoulders or wipe each other's tears. You weren't even supposed to touch your own face. Instead, the tears fell into your protective mask, where they collected and soaked until it was too hard to breathe.

My mom attended a lot of funerals that year. I looked down in the casket to see my grandmother, who had passed away that first summer. I felt my own throat begin to tighten, and I tried to put a hand on my mom's shoulder, but my arm passed through her.

I looked back down at the body, and it was my mom's best friend, my godmother, who was gone only a month later. My mom cried harder, and I noticed strangers walking around us, talking, and laughing, not even wearing black, like they didn't notice they were at a funeral.

"Mom, are you okay?" I tried to ask, but she didn't seem to hear me.

Couldn't these people see the body? It was still there, only now it was my aunt.

One of the strangers walked up to my mother and started up a friendly conversation about the weather. Another came with a clipboard and a form to sign. She continued to cry.

"Hello?" I said, but no one even looked at me. "What are you doing?"

A crowd formed around my mother, so many people that I could barely see the casket anymore. Little glimpses showed me that the body had changed again—I saw a flash of blonde hair, but then someone stepped in front of me, and it was gone.

"Hello!" I screamed, but the scene played on. The people talked, my mother cried, and no one even knew I was there. "Get away from her!" I yelled. "Stop pretending this is normal! Can't you see that she's going through something?"

The crowd was overwhelming. I could barely breathe. I felt myself melting into it, slowly disappearing until I was gone, nothing at all.

I jolted awake. *Something's wrong.*

My room was dark and quiet except for the sound of Emilia's soft breathing coming from her bed. I untangled myself slowly from my blankets. *Ew.* They were soaked in sweat.

I moved slowly through the room, trying not to trip on anything in the dark. *There.* My bookcase.

Most of it was used to store cosmetics and nail polish, but there were a few actual books too: textbooks, some trashy YA novels, and... *Oh.*

My diary was gone. Didn't I have a diary? I squeezed my eyes shut, trying to remember. I vaguely recalled soft paper pages and a leather cover—I had definitely *had* a diary. Where was it?

I grabbed my phone and pulled open the photos app, scrolling through until I found images from last summer. Except... There weren't any photos from last summer. *What the fuck?*

Why was there no record of those stupid months? Why couldn't I remember what had happened during them? And why, worst of all, did I want nothing more than to climb back into bed and pretend they hadn't happened?

I dashed out of the room and up to the roof. I yanked at the heavy door blocking my path outside way too quickly. My muscles groaned, but then I was outside. Fresh air. I ran away from the door, toward the stars.

"Are you okay?" came a sharp voice, agitated and authoritative.

"Ahhhhh!" I screamed, loudly, pushing all the air out of my chest.

"Shh, shh," I heard the voice shushing me, moving forward. Then there was one hand over my mouth and one around my arms.

I tried to scream louder, around the hand, but my shrieks of "Let go of me! Let me go!" came out as muffled sobs instead of words.

"Calm. *Down.* It's just me. It's Jordan, remember?" Hot breath accompanied the voice in my ear. "You have to stop screaming, or you're going to get us in trouble."

Jordan... Did I know a Jordan? How was I supposed to remember when he had me all freaked out like this?

"Ivy, we met on the roof a couple weeks ago, remember? I was out here when you ran through the door, and I wanted to make sure you were okay, but right now, I just really need you to stop screaming."

Jordan... The name clicked into place, and I let my screams die out. I squeezed my eyes tightly together. *Please let me go.*

He did. *Thank God.*

"Are you okay?" he asked.

I wanted to tell him that I wasn't okay; that it wasn't okay for him to go around grabbing people. But even more than that, I wanted to leave. "Yes," I said, "Thank you." I shuddered. I didn't want to thank him, but I really didn't want to make him angry.

"Any time," he smiled, showing off his perfect glowing white teeth.

"Goodnight!" I responded and ran back the way I had come.

CHAPTER EIGHT

IF I HAD DITCHED CLASS, I WOULDN'T HAVE ENDED UP IN THAT ALLEY

———

Ow. There was something hard pressing into my face. *Oh, it was my laptop.*

I had fallen asleep at my desk last night while trying to conjure an epiphany about why I was learning what I was learning in philosophy. It was Friday morning, a week after the toga party, and the first day of Halloweekend.

I got up and got ready for the day. I pulled on a black pleated skirt, a white blouse, black knee-high boots, and a gold and opal necklace with matching earrings. I gave myself cat-eye eyeliner and a frosty pink lipstick, spending extra time to make sure my face was perfect. *If I look perfect, I can't feel like shit. That's logical, right?*

When I examined the final effect in my mirror, I grinned. I totally looked like I could be a teen witch on the CW. All I needed was a wand and an inappropriate crush on an authority figure.

Halloween was my favorite holiday. It combined all the best things in life, like dressing however you wanted, partying, and lots and lots of candy corn. Plus, at Halloween the rest of the world seemed more open to exploring the fun unknowns of life, like ghosts and witches, the wild things I loved to believe in all year long.

I hadn't seen Chase all week, and I had spent more time than I wanted to admit trying to decide if I was happy or sad about that. On the one hand, I was furious. After he had abandoned me and told me I wasn't worth it, what gave him the right to just come back and hug me like nothing had happened? On the other, slightly more embarrassing hand, I was curious as to why he was here. So motherfucking curious.

I had always sort of accepted that none of last summer made sense. Every blog I read about how to get over a breakup seemed to confirm that men were elusive, brainless creatures who acted on their own impulses. Everywhere I turned, "I hate my ex" was a perspective that was validated and rationalized.

But now I was starting to wonder if last summer didn't make sense to me because it wasn't supposed to. Because there was a reason behind my memory loss... a reason, of course, which I couldn't remember.

I walked to my laptop to pack in my bag.

"*Why do you want to study philosophy?*" mocked the blank document before me.

"*I don't,*" read the only two words I had typed before passing out.

Philosophy was stupid. Why should I care what a bunch of old dead guys thought the meaning of life was? Most of them hadn't respected women, so why should I respect them?

Besides, I didn't *want* to keep asking questions about the nature of life. I was tired of being uncertain. I wanted things to make sense for a change.

Why couldn't I at least stick to *fun* mysteries, like whether the strange lights over the Potomac were just another helicopter or if they were an alien spaceship here to do research on our leaders, or what was on Floor K? Halloween mysteries, not awful ones.

A high squeak startled me from my thoughts. It was Whiskey. I smiled and went over to pet his head.

Fuck Socrates. I'm fine.

***

I had woken up early enough that even with the extra makeup, I still had enough time to enjoy my walk to class. I put on my trench coat and the six-hour playlist that Emilia and Will had made of all the music our friend group loved and pressed shuffle. The playlist included Taylor Swift for me, Billy Joel for Emilia, The Chicks for Will, the entire soundtrack to the movie *Baby Driver* for Harrison, and Kanye West for Aiden, mixed in with the dozens of songs we all loved. It was chaotic and wonderful, just like us.

I walked with one earbud out so that I could listen to campus around me too.

"I just think you lost some of the experience by reading a translation instead of the original Latin ver—"

"And I really had to pee, but some asshole was doing coke in the bathroom and he—"

"There's actually a lot that I don't understand about hostage negotiation," followed by a response in... *Norwegian?*

Campus was beautiful, as always: a pale blue sky and a world slowly transitioning to winter, with pumpkins scattered artistically around the campus. Ivy sprawled on the walls of old brick buildings, adding a splash of color to the ancient stone.

I loved it when the leaves turned right from green to red without any orange or yellow ombre nonsense in the middle. Just green to red, no transition phase at all. Like they were burning.

"Ivy?"

I froze.

"Ivy?" the familiar voice called again.

It was Chase. He had gotten a haircut since I had last seen him and was wearing his normal clothes again: kakis and a pale collared shirt. He looked like a preppy douche—but he looked like *my* preppy douche, the one I really knew.

"I have class," I said, and I tried to walk past him.

"Wait, just one second." He held up a hand to indicate that I should stop, but he didn't try to grab me.

I stopped, my curiosity getting the better of me. "What is it?"

"We need to talk," he started, his fingers twitching, the way they always had when he was overwhelmed.

"We *have* talked."

"No, we need to talk for real. While you're sober, while I understand what's going on. I need to explain."

"Explain?" I repeated.

He grimaced. "I've decided I can't explain everything that happened last summer, even if I wish I could. I can't tell you why you got that text from me, or why I left then, but…" His eyebrows pulled together as he struggled to get the words out.

"Ivy!" interrupted a cheerful voice. I turned and saw Harrison walking past and waving. I smiled and waved back, trying to pretend I didn't notice him raising his eyebrows at Chase and mouthing, "Who's that?"

I wasn't trying to hide Chase, not exactly. Wollstone was just so small, and rumors spread so fast. I didn't want to tell my friends my old ex was hanging around, and I especially didn't want anyone else to tell them. If any of them asked questions, I might have to admit that I didn't really have many answers.

I cleared my throat. "You were saying?"

Chase took a deep breath. "I don't know, exactly. I don't know exactly where to start. Do you remember—"

"Hey, Ivy!" He was cut off again, this time by two boys from my film class. Why the hell were so many people up this early?

"We're not talking here." I grabbed Chase's arm and pulled him off the main path to a narrow alleyway behind Gotland Hall. It was tiny and full of sprawling plants that had become overgrown just out of sight of the campus tourists. The ground crunched beneath us as we walked over dead autumn leaves.

"Ivy Bell, are you *ashamed* to be seen with me?" Chase asked, a look of mock horror on his face.

"Absolutely," I responded without humor. "And you have—" I checked my watch. "—sixty seconds to change my mind."

"How am I supposed to explain anything to you in sixty seconds?"

I looked pointedly at my watch again.

Chase looked around the alley, as though expecting a solution to appear out of the blue, then back at me.

"Okay," he said. "Okay, sixty seconds. I know what you remember about me doesn't help my case at all, but..." He trailed off and paused to take a step closer to me.

I froze, unsure if I wanted to move closer or step back. I wanted to know his side of the story, but he had already said he wouldn't tell me. *I had already walked away from him once before, and that hadn't gotten him out of my head.*

"Okay," he said again. "If I can't explain what I know, then tell me how you feel."

Now I stepped back. "How I *feel*? What is this, Chase—therapy? I see a professional for that."

"About me," Chase stepped forward again so that there was just a small space between us. "Tell me how you feel about me."

"I hate you," I said, trying to put some venom behind my words. I knew I hated him; he had no right to my love anymore. I'd just loved him for so long, was all. I couldn't get him out of my head because my head was used to him, like a drug or something. *Like that guy doing coke in the bathroom who wouldn't let that girl come in to pee.*

Still, I only moved one foot back.

He raised his eyebrows, sensing my hesitation. We'd been together so long; we had once known how to read each other. I'd once believed there was nothing he could do to surprise me, before he stopped talking to me all together.

Chase moved one foot forward. "I know you say you hate me, and I know why you think that, but you really believe it?"

I pushed back my other foot, and it hit the wall of the alley behind me. "I do hate you," I said, but I didn't sound as confident as I wanted to. I let my bag drop to the ground.

I thought back to my dreams, to my wandering mind this morning. *Who would I be if last summer hadn't fallen apart?* But no, I couldn't go down that road. I couldn't let him break me again.

"Are you sure?" Chase closed the final gap and leaned forward, placing his hand on the wall just above my shoulder.

My back pressed into leaves and stone as I tilted my head back to look up at him. I was very aware of the sound of my own heartbeat, rattling in my chest.

"I think there's some part of you, maybe just a small one, that still loves me," he said. "I think you've been trying to ignore it, but the feeling still has to be there."

"What does it matter if I love you? I hate you more." My voice shook.

He smiled. "We grew into love before, we could do it again. Don't you remember how awkward we were when we met? You were always saying, 'What if I had turned down a different street that day, we wouldn't be together now! We would be different people!' Well, maybe this is your if. 'What if I hadn't given you a chance, we wouldn't be together now!' Can't you see it?"

No. I couldn't. I wouldn't.

I remembered the pain of waking up alone with only his stupid text. I remembered the frozen headache that came with even just the thought of him. How I had first begun to worry about the *ifs* in the year of 2020, when everything was balanced so carefully, dangerously.

"I know you think you hate me now, but Ivy—"

I remembered everything before last summer, how complete I had felt when we belonged to each other. How he would buy me a flower every time he passed a cart on the street. How he made me feel as though I was important, worth caring about; when I was all alone and at my lowest.

I pulled Chase's head down to mine and kissed him. For a moment, he didn't seem to know how to react. Then he pressed forward, his arms on either side of me, pinning me against the wall. I pulled my hand through his hair and let out a soft moan as his mouth moved to my neck, then my collarbone, strong but still gentle. I lost myself in the time-lessness of it all, the way kissing Chase felt so familiar that he may as well have been a part of me, a crucial organ I couldn't live without.

Chase was starting to pull off my blouse by the time I came to my senses and realized how fucking stupid this was. I straightened and moved his hand away. He jumped back immediately, out of breath.

"Are you okay?" he asked, "Do you rem— I mean, why'd you stop?"

I shook my head, trying to clear it. "I shouldn't have done that," I said, panic edging into my voice. "I'm sorry. I-I don't know why I did that. I just... I mean, for a second I remembered how it felt when we were dating, and I just... Oh my god."

Why was I so fucking dumb? I had spent months hating Chase, based on logic and facts, but he came back for a week, and I let my hormones take over? Why had I done that?

I grabbed my bag from where it had fallen on the ground.

"Ivy, wait. Are you oka—"

"I'm late for class!" I yelled, which was only partially true, but who gave a fuck about honesty anymore? I ran.

***

I only made it to the last fifteen minutes of philosophy that day. I spent most of the period in the bathroom, splashing cold sink water on my face and using my emergency makeup kit to hide my flushed face. When I finally snuck into the auditorium, I pulled my notebook out as quickly as possible and pretended to take diligent notes in a flimsy attempt to prevent Will and Aiden from asking questions.

In the end I was saved, or possibly sacrificed, from talking to them at all when Professor Whitby called my name as she dismissed the class. I was actively shaking as I walked up to the front of the room, ready to be chewed out for being late again, but she only smiled.

"Miss Bell, I'm not here to punish you. I'm here to help you learn. I think you might be struggling to succeed right now, but we can get through it."

Was that professor for *I think you're falling apart?*

"I'm fine," I objected. "Really, I'm great! I'm working hard on my paper, and I've been getting plenty of fresh air and drinking water every—"

"You know you can talk to me, right?" she interrupted my babbling. "*Actually* talk? It seems like you have a lot on your mind, and I have office hours every week if you have any concerns you would like to address in a private setting."

Could I trust her? For a moment I considered it. Could I ask her why my dreams had been so terrifying, or why my parents were acting so shifty, or why my heart felt like it was constantly splitting in two?

"Thank you, professor," I said. "I'll stop by—to talk about my paper."

No, I couldn't be honest with her, not really. She would only think I was losing my mind, and I couldn't let myself go back to the psych ward. I would not go through that again.

I was so stressed about my kiss with Chase and my possibly impending insanity that I barely had time to be worried about entering the hospital as I made my way to Dr. Thana's office for therapy. Barely.

Instead, I felt numb as I walked through the sterile hallways, overwhelmed by anxiety, like when your toes get so cold that your body just gives up on telling you how much they hurt.

***

"How are you today, Ivy?" asked Dr. Thana in her neat, clinical voice. Her eyes were locked on me with their usual focus, as though she were committing every word to memory.

I opened my mouth to lie, to tell her everything was fine, but stopped cold at her raised eyebrows. It was like she could see right through me.

"I've been having some dreams." I went for a partial truth.

"Dreams?"

"Just-just the realistic dreams, like we were talking about." About a frozen laboratory. An endless funeral. "I fail a test, or throw up on a date, or I'm stuck in the elevator again." I feigned a shiver.

"And your real life?"

"Umm…" I trailed off.

Dr. Thana made a note on her clipboard, then leaned forward in her chair. Her glasses slid to the bridge her nose as she looked at me. "Ivy, therapy only works if you want it to."

I sighed. "My ex is in town."

Dr. Thana raised her eyebrows half a millimeter in what was likely the largest display of emotion I had ever seen from her. "The high school boy?"

I nodded. "And it's terrible timing, because I might be starting a new thing with this pretty girl. I mean, I think I might be starting a new thing. I'm not sure what's going on there, and I… I don't know what to do."

There, that was real. Another partial truth. Lots of girls have relationship drama, and that didn't mean anything. It didn't make me crazy.

"I was under the impression that you had bad blood with your ex?" clarified Dr. Thana, her eyebrows raising another half millimeter.

"I did! I mean, I do," I corrected. "I don't know. It's just... Well, it's confusing."

"Ivy, sometimes relationships are formed out of convenience. You've said yourself, the day you met that boy he was literally the only person on the street. It makes sense you would like him so much. Fifteen is a very hormonal age, and 2020 was a very strange year, but you don't need to hold a place in your life for him."

She was right. I had met Henley in a crowded room, and we had seen each other across the party. Meanwhile, Chase might have never talked to me if there was another girl on that street. Did that make it convenience? Or fate?

"Move forward, Ivy." Dr. Thana smiled. "Don't get stuck in the past."

CHAPTER NINE

IF I WERE A LIBRA, I WOULD BE GETTING LAID TONIGHT

———

The next day the five of us grabbed some blankets and sprawled out on the lawn between Lynum Square and Gotland Hall. The temperature in the district was dropping steadily as we marched toward winter, and the grass was full of Wollstone students savoring the relative warmth of our last fifty-degree day. The administration had even set up a farmers' market in the square; or, at least, the elite university version of a farmers' market, which included many artisanal food trucks and pressed juice stands, but not many farmers.

The sun was shining brightly over a pale blue sky, and the general buzz of chatter in the air felt energetic and good. I was happy. I was going to listen to Dr. Thana and move on from my past. I was going to invite Henley to a Halloween party tonight, and I was never going to think about Chase again. Everything would be perfect.

"...so really, it makes total sense that I'm a fire sign." Emilia picked at the grass. "Ivy, what element is your zodiac?" She and Will were sitting cross-legged, playing some game with a deck of cards and a wooden rectangle full of pegs. I was lying on the ground next to them, absorbing about half of their conversation. The rest of my mind was focused on the sky. My Russian workbook lay abandoned next to me, open to a page on verbs of motion.

"Umm..." I bit my lip, trying to remember if I knew anything about astrology. "I think Virgo is an earth sign."

Em made a face. "Really? Are you sure?"

"I think so. Why?"

"Aren't earth signs supposed to be, like, grounded?"

"Rude. I'm plenty grounded!" I sat up in indignation, too quickly, and the blood rush made me dizzy for a second. *Oops. Maybe I should start taking an iron supplement like Mom says I should.* I shook my head a little to clear it. "I mean, I am grounded. Right?" I looked to Will for support as the world spun back into focus.

"Will's an earth sign too, but *he's* grounded," Emilia interjected.

"Please leave me out of this," protested Will.

I turned my head back to look at Harrison, who was reading a book about the modern media's influence on free speech, and Aiden, who was entering his fifth minute of a plank. Neither of them said anything, but Harrison mouthed, "I'm sorry!"

Ugh. I knew they were joking, but the assertion hit just *slightly* too close to home. Losing memories and getting lost in dreams were definitely things that didn't happen to grounded people. *I could be grounded, though,* I told myself. *I could totally be grounded.*

"I'm going to go get a bubble tea from the farmers market," I said as I grabbed my phone and stood up, slower this time. A few leaves and blades of grass clung to my pink plaid skirt, and I brushed them off quickly. "Do any of you guys want anything?"

Will looked up at me from his cards, his face concerned. "You know she was only kidding, right? I mean, you might not be the *most* grounded person in the world, but that's not a horrible thing. Astrology doesn't actually mean anything."

"Careful with what you're saying, Will," said Em. "I learned a lot about being a witch from TikTok during the 2020 quarantine, so you probably don't want to piss me off."

"We're terrified." Despite the fact that Aiden was still planking and his arms were beginning to shake from the effort, he managed to deliver the line without any trace of an emotion in his voice. "We'll never say anything bad about astronomy again."

"Boooo," said Will. "Messing up the word 'astrology' is way overdone, completely unoriginal."

"Why should he be original?" I asked sweetly, batting my eyelashes and throwing my voice into the higher, more innocent pitch I used when I wanted a bouncer to let me into a club. "He was just taking an interest in our friends' passion for anesthesiology."

Emilia stuck her tongue out at me as she moved a peg on the wooden board.

Harrison flashed a big smile. "What element am I, Emilia? I want to learn about applied-sociology too!"

I mouthed "Nice!" at him, accompanied with a thumbs up. He beamed.

"So," I said again, my tone a little lighter this time. "Do you guys want anything?"

∗∗∗

As I made my way through the river of students to the bubble tea stand, I felt stupid. This was what we did. We told dumb jokes, and made fun of each other, and made stupid decisions together, and then made fun of each other for the stupid decisions too. Like siblings.

Remember not to worry so much about the past, I told myself. *Focus on the present.*

I took in a deep breath, inhaling the sweet scents drifting from the various food stands. I felt the cool air brush against my skin and tried to appreciate the last dregs of fall we would get before cold fronts set in. I listened to the conversations of students as I passed by.

"You know, I think I would go gay for Paul Ryan," mumbled a boy in an expensive-looking blazer, his forehead full of wrinkles as though he was very deep in thought.

"He told me it was his signature cocktail recipe, and then he just poured together a can of La Croix and a can of Natty Lite!" complained a tall ginger girl to her friend. "I have to stop seeing him, *right*? That's psychopath behavior."

"Was it awful?" asked a boy with big glasses, his voice full of what seemed to be genuine concern.

"No!" snapped his friend. "It was *wonderful*. I had the time of my life spending Friday night with my *toe* stuck in a *mousetrap*."

I brought my hand quickly to my face, trying to hide my laughter, but it was too late. Mousetrap-boy was glaring at me.

"Sorry!" I called, but he was already storming away. I thought about rushing after him to say... something? That I wasn't judging? That getting stuck in a mousetrap is totally something I would do?

But before I could take more than a few steps, my brain latched on to a different conversation.

"I literally don't know what she's thinking. I heard the blonde girl is, like, crazy."

"I know! She literally goes to the hospital *all the time*, and of course we both heard that she had an *enforced stay* last summer."

It was ironic, really, that for all the times on this campus when I couldn't remember a name or a face, my brain chose *this* moment to flawlessly recall the identities of these two girls.

Henley's friends.

These were girls who trailed after Henley, footsteps melting into sync with hers as they moved around the campus. She probably loved them like I loved Will, Em, Harrison, and Aiden. And they thought I was crazy.

"I heard the whole group has this, like, fuck bingo card, where each square is a different place on campus where they have to fuck someone. It's, like, a contest to get all the places first."

Okay, so that wasn't precisely right. Technically, we had made a bingo card with a list of locations on campus, but it wasn't like it was a contest. No one cared if you finished the card, or if you even really "hooked-up." Harrison and Rose had completed their card first, simply by going on a walk around campus and kissing each other once in each building.

And we had bingo games for lots of things, like buildings that we had cried in, dining halls you had gotten food poisoning from, or places you had taken a selfie with Wollstone's mascot, Waffle the Corgi. *Apparently nobody wanted to gossip about that, though.*

"Maybe that's what all the hospital visits are for: *STD screenings.*" They both laughed profusely at this, and I felt almost numb.

"Hey, hey!" I glanced back toward the girls and saw Henley joining them. "Sorry I'm late, I had to pick up a last-minute piece for my costume."

I turned quickly, slipping into the crowd before she could spot me. It had been stupid, really, to think about asking her out. I barely even knew her. We'd met twice, and that was only if she was telling the truth about the first time. Was she? I suddenly wondered, if Henley already knew about my trip to the psych ward last summer, if she wanted to see if I really was crazy by pretending we had met before.

Why did her friends even know about my psych ward stay? I had barely mentioned it since I got to Wollstone—I hadn't even let myself think about it. How had they found out? And why did it even matter if I went to the hospital or if we played stupid games to capture where our memories happened around campus? Couldn't people talk about their own lives? Did they really need to talk about mine?

I arrived back at our spot in the grass dejected without any bubble tea. Harrison had fallen asleep with his face in his book, and Aiden had switched from planks to push-ups.

I saw Will look me over, read my body language, and realize I was upset. But he didn't ask what happened or press me. Instead, he gave me half a smile and said, "Come be on my team. I'll teach you how to play cribbage so we can beat Emilia."

I relaxed, relieving the tension leaving my shoulders that I hadn't even realized had been there. Everything was going to be okay. I would still go to the Halloween party tonight, but it would be with my friends instead of a date. I should never have considered asking Henley out and getting close. If anything, I should be glad that I came to my senses before I really gave it a chance. This was a good warning.

I gave Will a small smile and sat down next to him in the grass. "Thanks, Will. I would love to."

***

"*Hey,*" the text that had just popped up on my phone screen read. *Unknown number.*

I wondered briefly if it was Chase before another message appeared. This one was longer, and I had to hold the screen just inches from my face to sort through all the words in the glow of the purple and orange strobe lights. We were at a party in a townhouse that the Wollstone Democrats, Republicans, and Bipartisan Coalition had rented out together and decorated as a haunted mansion.

Harrison and Rose had already split off from the group, the cowboy hats from their wild west couple's costume hovering over the crowd for just a moment before they disappeared completely. I hoped they had found one of the secret passages rumored to be in this house.

Will and Emilia stood beside me at the edge of the crowd. Aiden was hugging all of us, but he insisted it was "Not because I'm drunk but because I'm tipsy."

Normally, I would have dived in immediately, but today I wanted to survey my surroundings first.

I wanted to know what I was getting myself into.

"*Its henley!! I got your number from a friend in pride, hoope it doesn't seem like I was stalking you or anything haha, Are u at the politics party?*

I scrutinized the words. Was she texting strangely? Or maybe she was just drunk? Or maybe she made typos all the time, and I was reading into it too much.

"Everything okay?" Will had to lean down to ask me over the roar of the party. He was dressed up in a platypus onesie, as Perry from *Phineas and Ferb*. Next to him, Emilia was dressed as Shego from *Kim Possible*, with black and green leggings, a blazer, and a belt. Her hair hung loose in a dark wave. She looked awesome. Aiden was in a suit and sunglasses, carrying a thick pen like in *Men in Black*.

I was carrying a frying pan. I had on a little purple sundress and had spun my hair into a big braid full of flowers to look like—

"*Rapunzel!!*" came a new text from Henley. "*I see you!*"

I glanced around the room but couldn't spot her among the pulsing crowd of dressed-up students.

"*I'm a devil.*"

Then I spotted her halfway across the room, decked out in shiny red. She had on red thigh-high stiletto boots, a bright red dress with puffed sleeves and an A-line skirt, a pair of red horns stuck neatly in her curled black hair, and, of course, red lipstick perfectly applied and as bright as fire.

I panicked. I wanted to run away, but I wasn't sure how I could in this crowded room. We were in the main part of the townhouse, a big open space containing nothing but dancing people and a single, massive chandelier covered in fake cobwebs. There was nowhere to hide. And, even if I did get away, Em, Aiden, and Will would still be here. They might have questions if I suddenly disappeared. *Fuck.* I didn't want to spend the rest of my Saturday night explaining to my best friends that there were rumors spreading around the school about my sanity, or lack thereof. *And the rumors might be true,* I thought, and I immediately hated myself for it.

"Hey, hey!"

"Hey, Henley." I tried to smile, but it may have come across as a grimace. *Stop freaking out. It might be nothing.*

Will gave me a thumbs up from behind Henley, and Emilia beamed. Aiden lifted his head in a half nod, so small I nearly didn't see it.

"Would you want to go somewhere, to talk?" I asked Henley. I knew what people would think if I asked her to go somewhere private with me, but I didn't have that many options. I had to ask her about what I had overheard, and I couldn't do it in front of my friends.

"That sounds fun." Henley's perfect red lips pulled up into a smile, and I noticed, for the first time, that she had a small dimple on her right cheek.

See, Ivy, I told myself. *You really don't know her at all. You don't even know her face.*

I pushed myself away from the wall, away from the safety net of my friends, and into the crowd. I moved fluidly, finding gaps and using my elbows once or twice, not wanting to stop walking. I needed to find somewhere private, and the house was bursting with people. *Oh! Secret passages!*

I could find one. I knew I could. I had found some at Wollstone, and those were meant to be hidden. The secret places in *this* house were meant to be found, though. They were open secrets. They drove the rental price up and gave people a story to tell their friends about their weekend: a way to advertise the house.

Behind me, I heard a deep voice yelling, "Damn, girl. Did it hurt when you fell from heaven?"

"No," came Henley's quick response. "But I bet it will hurt when I cut your dick off with a pair of eyebrow scissors."

I snorted, amused by both her response and the fact that the required religion classes were probably doing their job if this douchebag actually knew that the classic angel pick-up-line was still *technically* accurate for a girl dressed like a devil.

I kept moving, made it to the wall on the other side of the dance floor, and passed through the first door I saw. *Perfect.* It was a library, with a low ceiling and a variety of lamps scattered around, providing just enough light to see. The walls were wrapped in gilded shelves, and each shelf was stuffed to the bursting point with books.

It wasn't exactly empty. The room had multiple antique-looking couches and big plush chairs, and several of them seemed to be occupied by embracing couples. Still, it was less crowded than outside, and a library was the kind of place to hide a secret door.

"Ivy?" Henley whispered in my ear. I jumped. I hadn't realized she was so close behind me.

"Yeah?" I asked without glancing back, as I began to circle the room, letting my fingers graze over book spines as I traced the wall.

"What are you doing? Or, what are *we* doing in here?"

I noticed the couples again. *Oops.* I should have explained, before we walked into the library, that I was not trying to hook up with her on a couch surrounded by people. *Or to hook up with her at all, especially when she seemed like she'd started drinking quite a while ago. Oh god, what if she thought this was for some bingo space? What if she thought I was a terrible person and might take advantage of her when she was drunk and I hadn't even started to feel tipsy yet?*

Don't think about it. She probably doesn't think that.

You just have anxiety!

Focus on the books.

There.

I saw a section of bright yellow covers, an old collection of Nancy Drew books. I walked quickly over and pulled on the second one, *The Hidden Staircase*. It tipped outward halfway until just one corner remained stuck between the books on either side.

Nothing happened. Maybe I had been wrong. I was seeing conspiracies practically everywhere, so it made sense that I would see them in a haunted house. Maybe the secret passages were made up for publicity and didn't actually exist.

Click.

The bottom section of the bookcase began to pull away.

"How did you…" Henley started to ask, but I put a finger over my lips with a glance at the library's other occupants. I really didn't want an audience. She nodded.

I ducked my head under the upper section of bookcase and crawled through the opening, frying pan first. I walked forward several steps, until I felt the tip of the frying pan bump into a wall. Behind me, I heard Henley's soft footsteps as she followed me inside, and then a *click* as the base of the bookcase swung shut behind her.

I began to reach around in front of me, where my frying pan had made contact. There had to be a light, or a candle, or something to make it less dark in here. It was starting to feel like that stupid elevator all over again: too small, too many shadows, too much unknown.

"Hey, Ivy?" Henley whispered.

"Yeah?" I whispered back. I wasn't sure if we needed to whisper any more. The walls could have been soundproofed or paper thin, and I wouldn't have known.

"What are you looking for?"

"A light. Like… like, maybe a lantern or candle or something?"

There was a beat of silence before Henley spoke again. I wished I could see her face, know what she was thinking. "Umm, Ivy, is your phone dead or something? Mine isn't."

What? "I don't think it is," I whispered. "Why?"

A longer beat of silence. This time, she only half attempted a whisper. "Ivy?"

"Yeah?"

"Our phones have flashlights on them."

"Oh, right."

And then, I couldn't help it. I burst out laughing. *Maybe I was wrong, and I was already tipsy too.*

There was a sudden brightness, and then I saw Henley standing a few feet away. Her lips were pursed together, like she was trying hard to keep from laughing too, but after one look at me, she broke.

"I *always*," I gasped, through fits of laughter, "forget about my phone."

"That's *so* random!" Henley cackled. "You can find a secret passage in a haunted house, but not your phone?"

"I have, like, eight hundred unopened text messages!" I pulled out my phone and looked at the little number by the "Messages" app. "Wait, I was wrong, it's actually eight hundred eighty-three!"

Henley closed the small distance between us in the passage, her arm brushing mine as she leaned down to look at my phone. "Oh my god, you really do. You're *insane*."

And just like that, I didn't really feel like laughing anymore.

"I'm not insane." I moved my arm away.

Henley's dark eyes flitted over my face, reading the tension. The inside of her left check pulled in for a moment, like she was chewing on it, before she responded.

"Of course you're not. Sorry, bad choice of words. I meant, like, weird, but I shouldn't have…"

"Did you talk to your friends about me?"

Her eyebrows pulled together. "Sorry?"

"Those girls, the ones that walk around behind you. I was at the farmer's market today, and I accidentally heard them talking… They were talking about me. About some rumors."

Her features looked, if possible, even tighter, but I couldn't understand what that meant.

Was she still confused? Was she about to yell at me for eavesdropping?

"Fuck!"

Okay, so that wasn't exactly a yell so much as an exclamation. I still didn't know if it was directed at me.

"Ivy." Henley turned toward me. She was so, so close, and with that closeness came the realization of how beautiful she really was. Henley wasn't just across-the-party pretty. She was gorgeous, like three-inches-away-with-an-iPhone-flashlight gorgeous.

This close to Henley, I could see that her cheekbones, while ridiculously defined, weren't sharp at all. They were round, like perfect circles lifting her face and forcing you to pay attention. She was wearing a devil costume and still could have passed for an angel.

And somehow, it didn't even matter. Henley Gara could have had the most average face in the world, and I still would have been drawn to her. Even if I had no idea why. I wondered, briefly, what had happened the first day we met. Maybe my subconscious still remembered. Maybe that was what was pushing me toward her.

"Ivy, I—"

"Wait," I blurted. "Wait. Maybe, if it's bad news, maybe you don't have to tell me. Maybe we can just pretend…"

She shook her head, slowly, deliberately. "I don't think it's that bad," she said. "At least, I hope not. But even if it was, you can't just ignore the things that upset you. You have to work through them before you move on."

I looked down at my sparkly purple heels collecting dust on the cold stone floor. "I don't like that theory," I whispered. "So, I'm just going to ignore it."

She laughed and then exhaled slowly. "I know you said you don't remember meeting me. Does that happen a lot, where you lose memories?"

I narrowed my eyes. "What does that have to do with anything?"

"It doesn't," Henley shook her head. "I mean, I was just thinking, and I'm definitely not a therapist so it's really just an idea, but have you ever wondered if you have such a bad memory because of all those memories you're repressing on purpose? Like, maybe your brain can't handle doing both at once."

"I'm not," I scoffed and paused. Something she had just said was pulling at me. *Not a therapist… Such a bad memory… All those memories you're repressing… Can't handle doing both at once…. Hmm.*

I tried to ignore the thought and started again. "I'm not repressing anything. There are just some things I prefer not to think about."

Henley lifted her eyebrows, which I was pretty sure was code for "I think you're wrong, but it's way above my pay grade, so I'm not going to get into it with you."

"Ivy, I did hear rumors about you," she began. "But I swear to you I didn't start them, or spread them, or believe them.

And they're not super wide-spread, or anything—just a few upperclassmen on the GCC board mentioned to me at the toga party. And by then I had already met you and really liked you. I mean," she stumbled, "not that I would have automatically believed the rumors if I hadn't met you, it's just—"

"What did you hear?"

"Umm…" Henley was chewing on her cheek again. "Are you sure you want to know?"

I nodded.

"They said you were forcibly admitted to a psych ward last summer. But I swear to you that I didn't tell anyone or believe or—"

"That's true."

She stopped talking. She looked me up and down and gave a small nod. "All of it?

I shrugged. "What's the rest of it?"

"Well, *why* you were in there. The boys said that you seduced a professor, and then things went wrong, and of course I know that would not be your fault because the professor would be in the power position and—"

"That part's not true."

Henley stopped talking again. She waited a beat, opened her mouth to say something, and then closed it. She repeated the cycle two more times before she finally seemed to find the right word. "Why?"

I looked back, confused. "Why what?"

"Why is someone spreading half a rumor about you? Why say something that's almost true and then…"

Something tugged in my mind. That was like the other rumor, about the bingo card. "Like my dreams," I whispered. "They're dangerous when they could be real."

"Sorry?"

"I need to go." Something was clicking into place inside my brain; something was starting to make sense where nothing had for months. *Half-truths.* "I need to go home."

"Oh." Henley sounded disappointed. "Yes, I mean, yeah. I'm so sorry. But really, I don't care why you were in the psych ward. That's your business, and I'll support you. My friends—they can be kind of bitchy sometimes. They don't mean it personally, it's just that they kinda want to rule the world someday, and they can get kinda wrapped up in power, reputation. I mean, I guess I can too, but I don't think you actually need a perfect reputation to get power. It's more about the opposite, right? Being charismatic *and* still making hard choices and doing unpopular things."

I didn't know what to say to that. The puzzle pieces that had begun clicking together in my brain paused, as if giving me a moment to try to work out what she was saying. But...

"I don't think what you just said actually makes sense," I said, squinting as though I could physically bring the meaning into focus.

She let out a tiny sound, a laugh, I thought. "I don't think it did either. I'm drunk, I'm saying too much, I'm saying the wrong things, I... I was trying to say that no one has a perfect past, and what matters more is how you are in the present. I was trying to say that I think you're charismatic."

"Are you sure that's not just hormones?" I blurted, and she gave a loud laugh this time. I joined in a second too late, trying to pretend it had been a joke and not something I was genuinely worried about.

I felt a soft pressure on my right hand and looked down to see Henley squeezing it with her own. "I'm quite sure. You're very likable, Ivy, and if I could get pollsters to come down and ask everyone at Wollstone about it, I'm sure the results would back me up. Rumors or no, psych ward or no, you're kind. People like that. I like that."

My thoughts were spinning, trying and failing to connect what Henley was saying now to what she had said before. I had to be missing some sort of crucial detail in this conversation, but I didn't think I had enough brain space to sort it out on top of the other questions I was trying to answer. I had to focus on one thing at a time, like she had been saying earlier. I had to sort out my memories first, and *then* I could flirt.

"Are we okay?" Henley asked hesitantly after my unresponsiveness had stretched into an awkward pause. "I mean, at least, still friends? At least?"

I nodded vigorously, even though I wasn't entirely sure she could see the movement in the dim light. "Yeah, of course," I said. "Friends." *Friends. Oof.*

But maybe, I told myself, trying to stave off a wave of disappointment, *not forever. The faster you sort your brain out, the sooner you can focus you attention on becoming... not-friends. Hmm.*

"Do you think that maybe, as my friend, you could do me a favor?" I forced myself to ask.

"Of course. What do you need?"

"Can you find my group, and can you tell them I'm safe but that I had to head home?"

Henley let go of my hand, and in the soft light I could just make out her dark brows pushing together. "I can, but... Are you feeling okay? Are you sure you don't want me—want *someone* to take you home?"

"I feel great!" I responded, which wasn't exactly a lie. I felt around the door that had let us into the passage until I felt my fingers clicking on a latch. The door swung open with the soft groan of an old house, and I ducked down to move through the opening, pausing only to give Henley one last small smile. "I just need to get home early tonight. I have a lot of work to do."

CHAPTER TEN

IF I HAD GOTTEN LAID LAST WEEKEND, I WOULDN'T BE STUCK IN AN ELEVATOR NOW

———

"Losing memories."

"Losing my mind."

"Losing my mind—'music video.'"

"Losing my mind—'music video'—'youtube.'"

"Losing you're mind."

"Show results for *'losing* your *mind'* instead?"

"Losing your mind."

"What to do if you think you might be losing your mind?"

"Can my university see my search history if I'm logged on to their Wi-Fi?"

"How to delete google search history."

I had never done so much research in my life.

Officially, if anyone asked why I was holed up in room 603 at noon on a Thursday, I was sick. It was the best excuse I could think of to avoid all my classes, appointments, and socialization for the fifth day in a row.

After I had made my way home from the Halloween party I had barricaded myself in the dorm to avoid distraction. I had been working nonstop, breaking only to eat the meals Em and the boys kept bringing me and to shower once a day so they wouldn't get concerned enough to call my parents.

I was worried that if I stopped for too long, if I let my mind get distracted by anything else, I would lose the tenuous grasp of understanding I had. Like a shark that had to keep swimming forward so she didn't drown.

I would not drown.

If I was losing my mind, I would fucking find it again.

So here I was, searching through medical papers I barely understood about the memories of depression patients, the side effects of my medication, the known long-term impacts of surviving COVID-19. I poured through every documentation I knew of from last summer, searching every social media account and every place I might have backed up my photos, every text, note, and email I had sent and received.

And after four days, when I had finally read everything I could possibly bear to read, I began to write. That's what had worked last time, last time when... When I had figured *something* out. *Last time...*

Somehow I knew that my answers, while frustratingly hard to reach, did exist. I had found them before, and I could do it again.

What Henley had said at the Halloween party had pulled the idea into focus. No, that wasn't quite right. It wasn't *what* she had said. It was *how* she had said it.

She had been giving me good advice, surprisingly good advice, actually, when she had said the phrase "such a bad memory" and pulled the page I needed to the surface of my mind. *My diary.*

I had written it during high school, when I began to sink into the depths of my depression. I had needed a way to get my worst moments out of my head, to stop replaying the dismal thoughts over and over, and I didn't have access to a ready supply of alcohol yet. I couldn't push them out.

So I wrote them down. *My diary.*

I could almost feel the journal in my hands now, the soft leather cover that tied up in a leather cord. I could practically smell the delicate creamy pages covered in layers of fresh ink. And I could see the first page, in which I had scrawled the title "Ivy's Book of Bad Memories" in looping cursive letters.

That stupid little book had begun as the desperate words of a struggling teenage girl, a way to physically close the cover on my least favorite memories and hide them away on a shelf. Then I had begun to organize it. Where my brain was messy, swirling, unreliable, and incomplete, I made the diary thorough and structured. I added dates and page numbers and seemingly insignificant details. I even wrote about the nightmares, described them as though they were memories too. And then, finally, after endless spent years and filled pages and worn pens, I found... *something.* Within all of that order, I had found my answers. I knew I had, even if I had somehow lost them now.

But I could find them again.

I sprawled out on a fluffy white rug on the floor of 603 with Whiskey sitting next to me enjoying pieces of fruit. I ripped out stiff pieces of college-ruled paper from my "Science for Future Leaders" notebook. *It wasn't like I ever took notes in that class, anyway.*

I reached over blindly to my backpack, grasping in the front pocket for a pen. *Dark green. Perfect.*

And then I stared at the blank page in front of me and told myself to write.

How had I started this before? I remembered my hand rushing across the page, so quickly that sometimes the ink didn't dry in time and left small stains between the words. *It had been easy.*

I thought back. I remembered being passionate about the moments I was describing, desperate to get them out of my mind and on the page. *Oh. Right.*

It hadn't been easy. I had been desperate. I had written quickly because I was frantic to push the memories from my head.

Okay, so I just had to pick a bad memory, one I wanted to get rid of. Hmm...

Writing down my least favorite memories meant *admitting* they existed in the first place. I had gotten used to ignoring them, skipping over the bad parts in my mind.

Okay. Maybe I could start with an easy memory, something recent that I hadn't had much time to push away. I pinched the bridge of my nose.

I could start with what happened on the way home from Halloween. I could handle that.

And then I put my pen to paper and let green cursive ink spread across the page.

———

Saturday, November 4.

It's cold, and I'm alone. I'm running.

I've just left Henley at a Halloween party, left everyone in my haste to get home. I didn't even think to call an Uber. Campus was only a few blocks away, and that distance seemed so short in my head. It had been short when I walked it a few hours earlier on my way to the party. The sun had been shining, and Emilia and I were with three college boys. (Em could probably take all three of them in a fight, and I could at least take Harrison, but that didn't matter to the men who passed us in their cars. All they saw were three boys, people to whom we belonged.)

Now, on the way home, it's dark, and I am on my own as a gust of frosty wind blows up the skirt of my purple dress. I am wearing spandex underneath, so I haven't revealed anything, but it doesn't matter. A pickup truck was passing, and its driver is already pulling over next to me.

"One more time, sweetie!" yells the man in the passenger seat as the truck slows down to match my pace.

I press down hard on my skirt, hands holding it firmly in place against the wind.

"C'mooon," groans the driver. "Give me another peak. It won't kill you."

I don't know where to go. I can't exactly get away from them—they have a motor vehicle. I glance around and see an alley to my right. Not the best choice I've ever made... But it's small enough that the truck can't follow, and I'm scared, so I go anyway. I can hear the men grumble in frustration as they realize they can't reach me in the alley and the rev of the motor as it resumes a normal speed.

I wish I had taken an Uber. I wish I had brought a taser. I wish I'd brought a football player. I wish I was stronger, that I had gone to the gym every morning and learned to lift the twenty-pound weights. I really, really wish I was stronger.

But I am so close to home. I will get to campus, I will take a hot shower, and I will get started on my plan to write and discover everything about my past. I am reaching the end of the alley; I can see a faint glow of lights from Wollstone's campus only a block and a half away. I am so close. I step out of the alley.

"Aayyy!" comes a deep yell.

I scream a little, but not loud enough to block out the sound of their laughter and calls of "Calm down, sweetie. We just want to be friends!"

They drove around the block. I was stupid, so stupid, to go in an alley. There was only one fucking exit! You absolute dumbass, Ivy.

I begin to run, my heels catching on the uneven cobblestones that line the sidewalk. They keep shouting, move their truck next to me, matching my exact pace, and I think I'm about to start sobbing when I hear a loud, incessant honking. Another car has come up behind the pickup truck, and this driver is mad. He blares on the horn, and I could scream for joy and hug him when the men in the truck give up, grumbling about how I'm not that pretty anyway, and continue down the street. I turn to look at the driver who saved me, to wave and thank them or something, but realize that the car is already moving down the street away from me, still tailgating the pickup truck.

Oh. I realize he was not honking for me but because he wanted the truck to get out of his way.

I take off my shoes and sprint the rest of the way back to Witt Hall. I take a hot shower and let it wash away my tears.

———

I set down the pen. I had written down more than I meant to. It had come so quickly. It had felt *so freeing.*

No wonder I used to write the bad memories down instead of just pushing them back. No wonder Dr. Thana had been trying to get me to journal. Between that and the advice about the most troubling dreams being the ones I couldn't concretely distinguish from memory, I was starting to wonder if maybe my therapist really knew what she was talking about.

I wonder what other adults have good advice…? I thought with a start. Maybe I should meet Professor Whitby for her office hours like she'd offered.

I decided to try another warm-up memory.

———————

Monday, September 25.

I am sitting in the doctor's office, actually in a chair in a basement room of student health, and he's refusing to test me.

I called. I made an appointment. I had to skip Russian just to make it to the appointment, and this man wasn't going to test me for mono.

"I just don't think it's necessary. I know it can be scary when mono is spreading around campus, but you don't even have a fever."

"But isn't there some sort of blood test or something you can run? Please?" I try my hardest to make the last word sound convincing.

The doctor sighs. "Ms. Bell, we would only need to run that test if we had reason to believe you might have mono."

I clenched my fists then slowly unclenched them and tried to keep the frustration from my voice. "Like I told your office when I made this appointment, and like I told you when I first walked in here: a girl I was seeing two weeks ago was just diagnosed with mono. Her doctor was the one who said I should get a test too."

"Ms. Bell, mono isn't as viral as some other infections. Just because your friend has it doesn't mean you caught it."

"I keep telling you, I'm not talking about a friend! We were sleeping together!"

Now the doctor looks confused. "Your boyfriend?"

"No, I don't have a boyfriend. I'm talking about the girl who has mono."

"Your friend?"

"Not! My! Friend!" I know I'm screaming, but I can't stop myself. "We were sleeping together. Two weeks ago, I was eating this girl out, and now she's been diagnosed with mono. So will you please, please test me? I've heard it can be dangerous, like, for your kidneys!"

The doctor looks taken aback. "Did you use protection, while you were... eating her out?" He makes a face as he says the last part, and I wonder what made him want to work at a college student health center, of all places.

"No," I say quietly.

"It is really much more responsible to use protection when having sex. Even if you can't get pregnant from, um, eating a woman out, you can still spread disease." His eyes dart over me, and his expression adds a final word to the sentence: obviously. "I've been saying for years that they should do more to make you kids pay attention during sex education in high school, to prevent problems like this down the road."

Was he being serious? "They didn't teach us about gay sex in school. They barely taught us about safe sex for straight people. Do you really think they spent a unit on how to safely eat a girl out?"

The doctor frowns even further and scratches a note onto a clipboard. "I have other appointments to get to. I'm going to send in a nurse practitioner to finish running your tests. Goodbye, Ms. Bell."

I sigh in relief and told myself that this would be worth it if it meant my kidneys wouldn't explode.

I kept writing, letting the lowest moments I hadn't let myself remember these last few months fall neatly onto the page.

I came up to the roof for peace, to breathe, but his hand is over my mouth and his arm is crushing my ribs. I can barely inhale at all as Jordan crushes me. I make a mental note not to go to the roof again.

"Anna, baby, you feel so good." His hands are on my chest, and I'm disgusted. I'm glad that I did not give him my real name.

"Please, this is weird."

"It's rude to disrespect the host, Anna."

"Anna! There you are girl," comes an excited voice. It's Henley, and she's walking straight toward me and the boy. "I have been

looking for you all night! Let's go get a picture over there," she says and leads me away.

I hear the boy cry out and turn to see him scowling in rage. I realize the pained sound wasn't because he was disappointed. It was because Henley stamped down on his foot with her stiletto as she led me away.

———

He is grabbing my wrists tightly, and something is very wrong.

"Why aren't you wearing a toga?" I ask, trying to plant myself in the pavement, forcing him to stop.

"What?"

"But we were at a toga party. Everyone else was wearing one. Why aren't you?"

"I came from another party, I didn't have time to change." Something else is wrong, because now I can hear an accent that he didn't have at the beginning of the night. Is it European? Have I ever seen this boy before in my life?

"Come on, I need to get home soon," he urges, the accent stronger now, and that worries me. If this is his real voice, why was he pretending to be American before, and worse, why is he revealing the lie now? Wasn't Criminal Minds always saying that when the bad guy starts giving you personal information about himself, that meant he wasn't going to let you go?

"Hey! Let her go!"

———

I stopped writing. This page, the one I had just written on, had started with Yona, with the two of us kissing, and then her going home. This page was the reason I had been out until two in the morning. This new diary meant that my missing memories were still there, somewhere in my head. I just had to find them, had to *want* to find them. I had to stop accepting half-truths.

And then, for reasons I still couldn't explain to myself, I pulled out a new page.

Friday, July 22.

Summer in DC is too hot, and the night air is damp and aggressive against my face as I walk from the doorway to the edge of the roof.

Wait.

I crossed that line out. I needed to start earlier in the night.

Friday, July 22.

Summer in DC is too hot, and the night air is damp and aggressive against my face as I walk from the doorway to the edge of the roof.

My legs wobble as I make my way up the single flight of stairs. The elevator hadn't had an option to take me all the way to the rooftop, so I had to settle for getting off at the sixth floor and looking for a stairwell.

———

That could not be right. I was misremembering that day. I had to be.

———

Friday, July 2.

Summer in DC is too hot, and the night air is damp and aggressive against my face as I walk from the doorway to the edge of the roof.

———

Friday, July 22.

~~Summer in DC is too hot, and the night air is damp and aggressive against my face as I walk from the doorway to the edge of the roof.~~
~~My legs wobble as I make my way up the single flight of stairs. The elevator hadn't had an option to take me all the way to the rooftop, so I'd had to settle for getting off at the sixth floor and looking for a stairwell.~~

———

When I finally found an elevator after wandering around this stupid medical labyrinth, it looked surprisingly ordinary. Old, *even. The carpet looked stained with something—beer, or maybe vomit? It was disgusting and entirely at odds with the sterile world I was leaving behind, but I didn't have much of a choice. I stepped on and glanced at the choice of buttons.*

How odd, I think. I would have assumed this was the lowest floor on the elevator's path given the underground, top-secretness of it all, but it's only second lowest, just above a floor marked "B." For Basement? I wonder before I remember that it doesn't matter and push the button for the highest floor I can see. "Six."

Holy. Fucking. Shit.

I knew exactly where to go.

***

"Hey there, Princess."

"Hey there, liar," I responded, not bothering to turn toward Chase as he approached me from behind the park bench. "I take it you got my text?"

"What have I lied about?" he sat down next to me, wincing a little as his skin touched the frozen metal. Winter was descending on the District of Columbia early this year, and we were expected to get *snow* soon. In November.

I let the denial hang in the air for a moment before I finally looked at Chase. He looked even better than the last time I had seen him. I stayed silent for a moment, simply drinking in the way he glowed in the starlight. His black hair shone, and every strand was gelled perfectly into place.

When we first met, I would make fun of how much product he used, both because he hadn't learned moderation yet and because I had studied sitcoms and thought that being a little mean was a good way to flirt. Then, we grew a little. My comments turned to lighthearted sorrow as I lamented how hard it was to run my fingers through his hair when we kissed. And then, I didn't say anything, because I decided that he was the most beautiful human alive, and I would want to kiss him even if he arranged his hair using the dirt and scum that floated in the Lincoln Reflecting Pool.

Chase's face was clean shaven, showing off the perfect cheekbones that shown through his golden skin. His nails had been cleaned and manicured, the ends forming the kind of perfect crescents that only seem to stay perfect on the fingers of the affluent. He wore his trademark peacoat over white pants, a tan Gucci belt, and a snow-white sweater that hugged tightly to his chest. I remembered the thousand times my head had rested on his chest. My cheek would press against angora fur, his arms would wrap around me, and I would feel shielded from every bad thing in the world.

"Ivy?" Chase cocked his head to the side, running his eyes over my face.

I sighed. "Do you remember the first day we met?" *That wasn't what I had planned to say.* I wasn't entirely sure why I had said it, but some part of me didn't want to get off that park bench just yet. "The street was empty that day. The world felt empty. Like it was just us."

"Of course it was empty," Chase said gently, and I wondered what was going through his head. Did he think I was crazy too? Or did he know the truth? Or, perhaps, was the truth that I was crazy?

"We met at the beginning of the pandemic, princess," he continued. "Everyone was staying away from each other. Everyone was scared."

"Yeah," I agreed. "We were pretty scared too."

"What's this about, Ivy?" he asked. "Why did you want to talk to me now? And why outside?"

"I just—" I paused. "Do you ever wonder what it would have been like if it had been different? What would our relationship have been like if there was no pandemic? Would we even have had one?"

"I don't know." He shrugged. "Why does that matter?"

"Can I trust you?" I asked, letting the urgency I felt echo through the question.

"You were the one who just called me a liar."

"And I'm still not sure that title was wrong," I responded. "But can I trust you *now*?" I wrapped his wrists in my hands and pulled him gently toward me until our faces were inches apart. "Please. I need help. You were one of my closest friends."

He grimaced at the word "were," but I kept going.

"You were right just now. It doesn't matter how it started, or how it ended, or what could have been. What matters is that before anything, *we were friends*. That was real, right? I need to know it was real. I need..." I trailed off and took a deep breath of November air. "I need a friend tonight. Can I trust you?"

Another puzzle piece clicked into place, another thing that had been missing for the past few months. *I didn't trust anyone. Not really.* I thought I trusted my friends until I reached the moment when I could have told them, "Guys, I think I'm going insane," but I didn't. Was it really because I didn't want to burden them? I suddenly couldn't be sure.

I really didn't trust myself. I hadn't for months. Ever since that day—when I woke up, alone with no idea why I was in a psychiatric ward—I had known deep down that I couldn't trust my memories. Ever since I started the medications and the strange dreams blew in, I had known that not everything I remembered was real. My own thoughts weren't to be believed.

Even worse, I didn't trust my own feelings. I hadn't for years, not since the depression started. It was its own kind of exhausting, fighting myself like that. Every time I wanted to cry, to break down or run away and just go and go and go, I had to question myself. Every time I felt frustrated, overwhelmed, or broken, I had to wonder if I was really reacting in the right way. Because every time I spiraled and went down that road—decided there was only one way out, the worst way out—it was the doubt that helped me survive.

But I had spent enough time doubting, and now I needed answers. I needed something to hold on to, someone to trust.

"Yes," Chase said after a few moments of silence.

"Yes… Yes what?" I clarified

"Yes, Ivy. You can trust me. Always."

I took a breath, and another. And then I smiled, *really* smiled, for the first time in days. "Then let's go."

***

The lobby of Witt was empty that night. It felt a little jarring, like missing a step at the end of the stairs. The lobby was never empty, not this late at night. Three in the morning meant girls covered in glitter and sweat from the club crossing paths with boys dragging themselves home from the library under towering stacks of books. Three in the morning meant people with epiphanies running off somewhere to write a poem crossing paths with the warm aroma of a delivery pizza.

But not tonight.

Tonight, three in the morning meant me and Chase on our way into the unknown, crossing paths with no one at all. It occurred to me that perhaps it was meant to be that way, that it was like a sign from the universe. Perhaps if I had seen anyone, I would have panicked and given up, pushed it off for another night down the road.

"Why are we here?" asked Chase, ducking his head a little as we walked past a security camera.

"You're fine," I told him. "We're allowed to bring guests here. If anyone's watching that feed, they'll just think I'm taking you up to my room."

He missed a step. "*Are* we going up to your room?"

"No." I kept walking without pausing to let him catch up. "We're going down."

"Down?"

We were at the elevator now, and I pushed the button once, gently. "We're going down," I repeated, and then I hesitated. I turned and looked at him. "Are you sure you can do this? You need to be sure, because I can't do it alone."

His dark brows furrowed, shading his eyes with concern. His face was pale, and his lips were pressed so tightly together that I could barely see them anymore.

"Of course. I want to help you, Ivy, but you're being all vague and cryptic. It's *weird*. Just, tell me, what are we doing here? Where do *you* think we're going?"

The elevator dinged open.

"Down," I said, pulling him inside. "To floor K."

There was no dramatic gasp, stunned silence, or anything that might have prompted a TV soundtrack to go *duh duh duuuh*.

"What is floor K?" Chase asked instead, glancing around at the tiny space.

I tried to imagine the elevator from his point of view. I wondered what he thought of the dried puke stains clearly visible on the outdated carpet. Did the dying lightbulbs hurt his eyes the way they had hurt mine in the first few weeks here?

I forced in a deep breath and pushed the button just below K, marked "B" for Basement.

The elevator started descending slowly, with it's awful groan, and I began to count in my head: *One... Two... Three... Four... Five... Six... Seven... Eight... Nine...*

The doors opened with a small *ding*, and we were in the basement. Chase started to walk off the elevator, but I swung out my arm to stop him. "We're not getting off yet."

I heard him sigh and mutter something under his breath. *Was he getting impatient? Would he leave?* Only six months ago, I knew him—really knew him. I could read every facial expression, understand every minute change in his body language. I knew that he liked pineapple on his pizza, that he hated orange, and that he had never once in his entire life woken up before noon on a Saturday.

Now, I investigated his beautiful, stupid face, but I couldn't read it. His nose could have been wrinkled in annoyance, confusion, or disgust. His eyebrows could have drawn together in worry, concentration, or frustration. I didn't know him anymore, and it was like I had lost an extension of myself, like when you first cut your hair and keep running your fingers through where it used to be. Maybe if I waited long enough, if I kept at this, our friendship would grow back. Maybe.

I shook my head to clear it and forced myself to turn away from Chase as I hit the button to the main floor. The elevator began to move, and I began to count.

One... Two... Three... Four... Five... Six... Seven... Eight... Nine... Again.

The doors slid open, but I could only see the lobby for a moment before Chase was blocking my view. He was standing so close to me that my nose was almost touching the collar of his shirt.

"Ivy, this has to stop. Go to bed."

"Chase wait, just—"

"You're not making any sense, and I'm worried about you. I think everyone is worried about you. Please." He stepped forward as he talked, and I stumbled to the back of the elevator. The scent of his cologne, bergamot and smoke, wafted over me, and for a second it felt like nothing had changed.

"No." My voice was solid, not shaking for the first time that night. "I have a plan." I took a step forward so that we were pressed together. "If you trust me, if you really want to help, then stay. I just need you for four and a half seconds. Please."

Chase nearly rolled his eyes, but he stayed. "Four and a half seconds?"

"I'm going to send the elevator to the basement. We're going to wait four and a half seconds, and then we're both going to jump. If nothing happens, then we'll both go to bed. I promise." I huffed. "I know it sounds crazy, but you said you trust me."

I lifted my pinkie, and after a moment he linked it with his own.

"Okay." He turned away and pressed B on the keypad. "Let's do this."

We counted together this time, and it felt a little silly, like were little kids. "One, two, three, four, jump!"

We grabbed hands, and for a second we were floating, hanging in the air.

And then we landed, tumbling into a heap on the floor as the elevator began to shake and sputter. There was a horrible shrieking noise, for just a second, and then... Everything was silent and still.

"Are you fucking kidding me?" Chase yelled, and I realized with a jolt that our faces had ended up right next to each other. "Did you know this would happen?"

"Umm..." I responded hesitantly and began feeling around on the floor for my bag. "Technically, yes?"

"You knew we were going to crash? And you did this anyway?"

"We didn't crash!" I objected, finally locating my bag and pushing my hand inside. "We're just... kind of... stuck."

"Why would you trap us in an elevator? We could have died! Why didn't you just, I don't know, ask to get coffee or something?"

I ignored him and chose to focus instead on what was in my bag: a hairbrush, a tube of lipstick, a condom, a bag of gummy worms, and finally, of course, a crowbar. Perfect. I pushed myself off the floor and held out a hand to help Chase. He didn't move except to cross his arms in protest.

"Come on, Chase. We don't have much time. If we're going to do this, we need to do this before the police show up."

"What is 'this'?" He wasn't asking so much as shouting. "I'm not moving one more inch until you tell me what's going on."

I sighed and turned away from him. I could deal with him later, one problem at a time. I slipped the crowbar between the doors and pulled.

And gasped.

I stumbled back a bit, tripping over Chase.

We hadn't timed it perfectly, so the elevator wasn't quite in line with the hallway in front of us, but it was enough. I could see it, hanging just a few feet above us. It was real.

Floor K was real.

CHAPTER ELEVEN

IF I HAD DONE YOGA INSTEAD OF JOURNALING, I WOULD NEVER HAVE GOTTEN MY MEMORIES BACK

—

I had been in underground tunnels before; I had been in hidden, *undiscovered* underground tunnels before. I had smelled the old cigarettes, the must, and the rot. I had tripped over loose bricks, gotten scars from shards of ancient glass bottles, and ruined perfectly good dresses from dirt and dust. I knew exactly what the underbelly of my school looked like.

And this wasn't it.

The hallway could not have been brighter if we were on the sun. It looked and smelled as though we had just walked into a giant bottle of bleach: pure white and... chemical. There were no windows, no exit signs, not even a single scuff mark on the blank tile floor. And it was cold—so cold—so much colder than it had been outside.

The halls were compact, but they seemed to stretch on forever. Chase had to bend his head just to keep from hitting it on the ceiling. Even I could have touched both walls with my arms if I bothered to stretch them out. Somehow, all the light and emptiness made it feel smaller, or at least made me feel more claustrophobic. Maybe that was why Chase looked so incredibly pissed.

I had kind of thought that, if I was right about floor K, if I found a real, physical place that matched the conspiracy in my head, then I would finally start to feel sane again. I had imagined that once Chase saw what was on the secret, underground floor beneath my building, he would be totally onboard team Ivy-isn't-crazy-after-all. I was wrong.

We had been wandering through this fluorescent maze for about five minutes now, and all he had said, repeatedly, was, "This can't be happening. This *can't* be fucking happening."

I ignored him for the most part. I was trying to focus on the strange setting around us, to force it to find a place in my head. If I had remembered *where* this creepy tunnel system was, shouldn't I be able to remember why it was here or how I knew about it?

"Ivy, can we please go?" Chase's voice cracked a little, and his boat shoes were squeaking on the floor. "Can we just, I don't know, go sit in the elevator and press the help button?"

"No!" I said firmly as we reached a crossroad, and I decided it was time to turn. I had been trying to keep track of every turn in my head, but it was impossible. We might have been on our seventh or our seventy-third twist. I wasn't really moving strategically, but still... I didn't feel lost. It wasn't déjà vu, not exactly... It was something just a little bit offset—like meeting a celebrity in person when you've only ever seen them in movies before. It felt recognizable but too unreal to be entirely familiar. *Spooky.*

"Ivy, if you don't turn around soon, I'm leaving without you. I'll use the elevator's emergency button and call the police."

I sighed. Why was Chase acting like this? Why had he agreed to meet me in the middle of the night on a random park bench if he was just going to give up when things actually got interesting?

"Fine," I said, trying to keep the hurt out of my voice. *That probably didn't work.* "Leave. But I'm staying. I need to know what's here. I can't explain it, Chase. This place *feels* familiar. I need to know why."

"No, you don't!" He wasn't even trying to stay calm. He stopped walking, and I did too. "You don't need to know everything. No one does. You have a really great shot at life up there, Ivy," he said, pointing up toward the ceiling and the outside world. "Can't you be happy with college and your friends? Why do you have to go chasing after secret laboratories and slimy fish tanks?"

I froze.

"What did you just say?" I whispered.

"I said, we need to go!" Chase was looking down at me, pleading with his eyes.

"You said, 'a secret laboratory,'" I said slowly. "And a slimy fish tank. Why did you say that? Why did you say it was a laboratory, Chase? Why a fish tank?"

He froze too. "I think... You told me?"

"No!" I said firmly. "I didn't. So how do you know?"

Chase said something through his teeth. It sounded like it was either a curse or a prayer. I tried to turn away to run down the hallway, but he was faster.

"Fuck it," I heard him mutter under his breath, and then he lunged for me, threw me over his shoulder, and started to run.

In all our years together, I had never really thought of Chase as the toxic masculinity, manhandling, kidnap-y type.

I had never bothered to wonder which of us might win in a fight. I had never needed to consider this.

Chase was taller than me, stronger than me, and he had all that pent up aggression that boys get when their parents aren't around quite enough.

But right now, I was more determined. I was more pissed off. And, of course, I still had a crowbar. I swung.

"Ow!"

To be fair, it wasn't like I went for his face or anything. And really, I didn't even hit him that hard. I had simply given Chase a nice little tap on his left leg with the crowbar, and honestly, it wasn't my fault if I had a lot of adrenaline coursing through my veins. Still, I tried not to listen to his screams of pain as I ran away from him and into the unknown. I tried not to notice that the sound he was making was the same one he had made in the COVID-19 ward three years ago, when he had already begun to recover and it had seemed like I was about to flatline.

I did exactly what I always did: I ignored it, and I moved on.

My path through the tunnels seemed more instinctual now that I was running and all hopped up on that just-been-kidnapped energy. Every time I got to a potential turn, I knew exactly where to go, as though the correct path was slightly colder or slightly brighter than the other options. I ran, and I ran, until I was pretty sure I would just drop dead right there if I ran any further. *Maybe I should take up jogging soon.*

And then I turned a final corner, and I saw it—the metaphorical light, at the end of the very literal tunnel. The room from my dreams. It was right in front of me.

It was real.

The laboratory was situated on the opposite side of a set of glass sliding doors. It was exactly as I had dreamed it, only with sharper edges and more of an emotional punch to the gut. The lab was there, an underground two-story room full of strange medical instruments, huge fish tanks, and pads and pads of notes in that stupid doctor handwriting that no one else could really read.

How had I known this was here?

If my stupid brain had some hidden goddamn GPS that could lead me here, then why didn't it have a welcome brochure or something? *What exactly was here?* I started to look around.

The room was big, nearly half the size of my high school gym, only not as tall. I guess that made sense, since we were underground and all. Despite its size, it was jam-packed and completely overwhelmed with random, vaguely scientific-looking instruments and machines. I might have called it cluttered if it wasn't all so futuristic.

Cluttered just didn't seem like the right word, though, not for something so bright, clean, and modern. And, despite how crowded the room felt, it still seemed organized. Like, whoever put all this stuff here could probably walk in and find anything they needed on the first try... like the way my desk drawers looked to anyone except me.

Looking closer, I noticed there were mirrors everywhere, big and small. *Why the hell are there so many mirrors?* I cared about my makeup more than anyone I knew, so if *I* thought they were going overboard with the mirrors, that was really saying something.

I started to wander around. I moved slowly, worried I might topple one of the tables full of beakers with neon goo or stacks of handwritten notes piled up higher than my head. Occasionally I stopped to pick up a clipboard of strange diagrams of the human body, examine a vial labeled "scopolamine," or try on a pair of headphones that muffled sound so completely I couldn't hear myself even when I tried to shout. Mostly, though, I just wandered, waiting for something to happen, for everything to start making sense. And then I reached the far edge of the room and found the fish tank.

It wasn't exactly a fish tank. It was human sized, with the word "Pandora" carved into the frosty glass, and instead of water it was full of a smooth gel. I tried to poke the gel, obviously, but it was so strangely warm that I pulled my hand out almost immediately. On one side of the glass tank, strange tubes and wires were sticking out in a thousand directions, connecting it to some of the weird devices of the room. I followed one, tracing it with my eyes, and saw that it led to a heart monitor with a screen that was currently showing a flat line.

Who could possibly be using this room? Was it aliens, or some secret society? What were they using it for?

How had I known about it?

I turned again and saw something else from my dreams: the steel table. There was no sheet covering it now, no immobile body, so I could see it had four small cuffs. One for each arm and leg. *What the fuck? Definitely aliens.*

And then I saw it, layered among a stack of textbooks nearly as tall as I was, standing in a precarious stack on the floor. Small, black, and leather: my diary.

Oh my god. My diary was here, in the creepy underground lab. *What would aliens want with my diary?*

I grabbed the little book, not bothering to move all the books balancing above it in the stack first. The whole thing toppled with a crash, but I didn't care. I unwound the little leather cord and opened the cover.

Ivy's Book of Bad Memories.

I flipped to the next page and recognized an entry I had written in the tenth grade.

Most people think that depression is just being sad all the time, but I know they're wrong. Depression isn't sadness, it's waiting.

You withhold things from yourself and tell yourself that you'll be happy if you get a boyfriend, or you'll love yourself if you lose ten pounds, or your life will mean something if you pass the right test, or get into the right college, or get the right job.

You wait. And you wait. And you wait to feel better. But then you get the boyfriend, and you lose ten pounds, and you pass the test, and you're not better.

You're just... older.

I remembered writing that. It had been years ago, scribbled out in a sort of desperate frustration.

I began flipping through the pages, skimming the moments of my high school despair.

———

Three days ago, in the hallway at school, I was walking past, and a group of boys started whooping and asking for my number. I said no. They started yelling at me, angry, telling me that I was "ugly anyway" and moving toward me in this sort of frightening mass. I told a couple friends what had happened, and they said, "Well, of course they got angry! You're supposed to just give them your number, and then you can just block them later if you need to."

———

Oh.

———

So that's why, today, when I was waiting for Aribella after school and a different boy asked for my Snapchat, I smiled, was friendly, and said yes. He decided to hug me in the school hallway, and I did not like where his hands landed. And you'll never believe it, but when I told some friends about what happened, they said, "Well, of course he thought he could hug you! You gave him your Snapchat!"

Feeling very confused.

———

Today, one of my friends came out to me as bisexual. I am so happy for her, and I love her very much and will support her. But also, I've been thinking...

Okay, so I feel crazy writing this, because I have a boyfriend. I have Chase, and I love him so, so much. I don't want to date anyone else, just him, so how can I be wondering now if I'm bi too? Is that cheating to even think that?

Obviously I knew what being gay was before now. I just also knew I wasn't gay, because I loved Chase, and I'm definitely attracted to men. But honestly? I never even considered being bi. Like, I feel like people don't even talk about it, or if they do it's like this weird stepping point before you're finally ready to come out as straight.

But... I think I might be. I'm not sure, maybe it's just a phase or something, because again, I love Chase so, so, so, so much. Like, I might spend the rest of my life with him, once we're not sixteen. But honestly? I don't think I've ever really cared about gender. I think I've always loved women too, just in a more confused and repressed sort of way because I didn't understand it. I would love Chase as a woman or a non-binary person. What if gender just... doesn't matter? What if I can just love anyone, find anyone beautiful?

If someone is kind, funny, and good to me, why would it matter what gender they are?

Oh god, okay, this is weird. I guess this is all hypothetical anyway. I have a boyfriend, who I love, so maybe there's no point in even thinking about this. Hmm. Will come back to this later.

———

I don't know how to talk to my parents anymore. I love them so much, but I never know what to say, how to act. I feel like I'm performing as Ivy in a play, trying to remember my lines, trying to remember how to act happy when I feel... numb.

But I don't even know why. What gives me the right?

I go to a good school. I have friends and a boyfriend and parents who love me. My life is wonderful, I have so much privilege, so why do I feel so shitty all the time?

And how would I even tell my parents?

"Hey, Mom! Remember how you triple majored in college while you were constantly working to pay for it yourself? Well, sometimes I feel overwhelmed at the prospect of answering an email."

"Hey, Dad! Remember all those years and years of grueling medical school you went through to save lives and provide for us? Well, last Friday I had to present a diorama about the nineties and take a calculus test on the same day, and last Thursday night I was so stressed I couldn't stop hyperventilating."

"Remember how you guys have loved me and given me everything for the past sixteen years? Well, apparently, it's still not enough. I'm miserable."

I flipped forward through the book, anxious to get to the end. A page fell out.

For a second, I watched it float gently down to the floor of the lab, remembering... *almost.*

So, I picked it up.

Friday, July 22.

Dear Chase,

I'm so sorry to leave you here, but I knew you would try to stop me.

I've felt wrong, confused, for so long now. I know now that part of it is because of this stupid Pandora nonsense we found today, but part of it isn't.

I feel like I'm all these contradicting things, and yes, I know now that one of the contradictions is being myself and not, but it's everything else too.

Like, for example, I know I'm so lucky to be pretty. I know people are nice to me because of it, that they give me extra chances and the benefit of the doubt and other advantages in life. Hell, I like being pretty, I love getting dressed up and doing my hair.

But I also don't feel like my body belongs to me. I feel like it belongs to the group of construction workers yelling at me on the street, or the grown men who stare at my ass, or the boys who touch me in the hallway, like I'm just this thing that belongs to other people, and it's so... gross. I wish I could be invisible.

Or like, here I am, always wondering if I am good enough, thinking about moving up in life like my parents did and providing my own kids with an even better life than mine.

But I also know I will never feel like I am good enough.

And now? Now that I know I should be dead? That I'm not really here?

I can't do it anymore. I'm sorry, I'm just not strong enough. (Maybe iiivy will be.)

I love you, so much, and tell my family I love them too. I've spent years feeling broken inside, and maybe it's been three years too long. But the moments with you? They made it all worth it.

I hope you find someone wonderful, someone who can stay.

Goodbye, cruel world. Again.
iivy

Huh. *Again.*

I had written this note after I discovered the lab the first time. I had written it and left Chase here and gone to find the elevator. I had written it and gone up to Witt Hall, before I ever even lived there. *But how would I know it was there, then? Because… I hadn't been planning to go to Wollstone last summer, had I…?* Back then, I was planning on attending Vanderbilt.

Okay, so I had written this note, and then gone up to the roof and tried to jump, only… someone had stopped me? Or something? I had woken up in the psych ward without so much as a scratch.

I had tried to jump. I skimmed back over the letter, my eyes latching onto the last line.

Goodbye, cruel world. Again.
iivy

Suddenly the memory slid into place. I saw flashes of my past. I had written this letter. I had gone to the roof.

I had gone up to the roof to jump.

"Ivy?"

I jumped at the sound of Chase's voice from only a few feet away. I had forgotten that he was down here, lost in reading. He must have found his way through the tunnels.

"Are you… crying?" he asked cautiously.

I touched a finger gently to my cheek, and it came away damp. "Yeah," I murmured. "I guess I am."

He came toward me slowly.

"You know?" he asked, and he didn't look angry or frustrated anymore. He looked determined.

I shook my head. "I'm not sure. I think so."

He gingerly wrapped on arm around me. "Do you... know?"

I snorted. "I take it that means you know too?"

"Ivy?"

"Yes," I sighed. "Yes, I know. I died."

Chase sighed and squeezed his arm around me tighter. Then his other hand came up, and a damp cloth smothered my nose and my mouth. I tried to yell, to fight, but he held me firmly, keeping me in place as I struggled, holding the material against my face, forcing me to breath it in until there was no fight left in me and every muscle sagged in exhaustion. As I let my eyes close and my body sink comfortably into his arms, I heard him sigh.

"I never wanted you to find out."

CHAPTER TWELVE

IF CHASE HADN'T BEEN WEARING HIS GUCCI BELT, I COULD HAVE ESCAPED BEFORE THE WHOLE MONOLOGUE

———

I awoke in utter bliss. I was lying in something cool and soft, like a cloud. The world around me was quiet and fresh, entirely lacking the faint smell of vomit and marijuana that normally soaked through Witt Hall. And, best of all, I had dreamt no eerily lifelike dreams.

If I had one complaint, though, it was that my wrists were bound together tightly, just above my head. *Hmm.*

I opened my eyes.

The room was well-furnished but impersonal. A hotel room. Pale beige curtains covered all the windows, and only one ray of sunlight had managed to fight its way through, casting my surroundings in the dimmest of glows. My body was covered by a thick, white comforter, and my hands were tied to the bedpost behind me by a leather Gucci belt.

"Chase!" I yelled, my mood ruined. "What the *fuck* did you do to me?"

I heard a thumping noise to my left and turned my head just in time to see a lamp roll off a table, next to where Chase was scrambling to stand up.

"You're alive!" he beamed. "I was so worried I had used too much—you've been passed out all night."

I glared at him. "I'm not *really* alive though, am I? That's why you drugged me and kidnapped me, right? That's why you've been acting weird since last summer? Because I died?"

The smile fell from his face, and he took a slow step toward me, as if he were approaching an orphaned fawn in the woods. "Not... Not exactly. What do you remember?"

I wanted to yell at him again, for drugging me, for lying to me, but not as much as I wanted to understand.

"There was an underground laboratory, beneath my dorm." I took a breath and shut my eyes, picturing it. "There was a room. I had seen it before; I'd been dreaming about it, with strange machines and tables full of data and a cold, metal table. I remember lying on it. It all looked so familiar, and then I found my diary, and it had all these memories that I had forgotten. And there was this letter... to you..." I faltered. "It said I wasn't me anymore—that I—"

He took a deep breath in and paced to the other side of the room. "Are you sure you want to know?"

For one, stupid moment, I wasn't sure. *Maybe*, I thought, *I don't have to know. Maybe I can just go back to my friends, to fun and freedom and parties over the Potomac.* But then, denial had never really worked for me long-term, had it?

"I want to know."

Chase closed his eyes and pinched the bridge of his nose like he was searching for the right words. Then he turned to me, met my eyes, and said, "Ivy Bell died in 2020. Complications from the coronavirus."

"But—" I interjected, unable to stop myself, but Chase kept talking as though I hadn't said anything.

"Ivy Bell died again, last summer, in 2023. She jumped off a rooftop. I guess it was the roof of your dorm."

"So how—"

"In 2020, the US government partnered with researchers at Wollstone University Hospital on a last resort project to save certain influential patients from the coronavirus. It was expensive and complicated and incredibly top-secret, but it worked. And when Ivy Bell died, her mother, who was the one who had negotiated the terms of the arrangement, and her father, who had pioneered the research, threatened to pull government access to Pandora unless they could use it to bring their daughter back."

Here, he finally paused, waiting for me to speak.

I wasn't quite sure what to say. My parents were still haunted by that year, overwhelmed by the magnitude of the pandemic. They had seen horrible things, but they had saved *so* many people. Or, at least, I thought they had.

"What's Pandora?" I asked, my voice sounding very small.

Chase bit his lip. "It wasn't originally meant for a virus. Your dad and one of his research partners had been working on it for years. I think it was originally supposed to replicate healthy tissues to fight cancer or something, but then they realized it could replicate far more. Your mom was the one who saw its potential and—"

"What *is it*?" I asked again.

"Do you remember that glass box from the lab? The one with the goo?"

"*Chase*," I said, tears beginning to well in my eyes. "Just tell me."

"They cloned you." He let it hang in the air for a moment before adding, with an almost apologetic expression, "Twice."

I wanted to tell him he sounded stupid. That that was impossible. But... I could feel it. He was right.

I remembered, suddenly, my dreams, or memories, or whatever they were. I remembered the metal table, a sheet covering a small body. I remembered the casket with a flash of blonde hair.

My body. My casket.

"So," I began, before I knew exactly where the sentence was going. "So, is everyone from that hospital a..." I couldn't quite say the word, but Chase knew what I meant.

"No, no, not at all," he said. "First of all, it's ridiculously expensive to create a human being from scratch. Second, it would have been such a mess legally to clone people without permission, and the government wasn't really ready to announce they had the technology in order to *ask* for permission. So, aside from you, it seems like they only used it for really important government assets, like President Hillmore."

"The president died?" I asked.

The president of the United States is a clone.

Chase bit his lip again. At this rate, it would start bleeding soon. "I think... I think the prime minster of the United Kingdom too. The powers-that-be in the government decided that their leaders dying during a global pandemic might, you know, destabilize things, so when someone was too sick— when they couldn't be saved—Pandora created a new, healthy clone with the same age and memories and everything as the original. Then, when the original died, the bodies were switched. *You* were switched."

I tried to remember the first time I died. I thought I had started to recover from the coronavirus back in 2020. I expected some memory of waking up, feeling brand new, but there was nothing. I had been exhausted, my lungs aching from the coughing and the fight to breathe. More and more machines had been connected to my body, supplementing the vital tasks I had once taken for granted, supplying me with water, oxygen, and drugs. Then, slowly, the weariness had worn off. At the time I thought I was healing, winning the fight against the virus in my body, but now I wondered if they had simply been weaning me off sedatives. *Or maybe that was what it felt like to come to life.*

I knew exactly when it must have happened the second time I died, the time I jumped. I had woken up in a room at the end of the hall in Wollstone's psych ward, dressed in an itchy cotton gown, no makeup on my face or polish on my nails. I had felt strange, alien in my own body as I stood up from the hospital bed, unsure of my footing as I left my room to seek out a doctor and ask what the hell had happened.

They had told me that I tried to jump off a rooftop. But that was just another half-truth, buried among my memories. *Tried. Ha.*

And then I remembered a conversation with another patient, a creepy older man whose lingering gaze had made me wish the material of the hospital gown was *just a tad* thicker. "When they wheeled you in here," he had said, "I thought you were a goner for sure."

He had thought I was dead. *I guessed technically I was—I just didn't stay that way.*

I was suddenly overcome with the urge to giggle.

"Do you remember those books I used to read?" I asked Chase. "The murder mysteries, Agatha Christie, and the like?"

He nodded, and I realized he had walked over to the edge of the bed while I lay lost in thought. "You read *And Then There Were None*, like, a dozen times before the pandemic calmed down and we discovered clubbing."

"This is kind of like a reverse murder mystery," I said, unsure why the concept struck me as so hilarious. "Usually, the characters try to figure out who the killer is, but I know what killed me. I just didn't know who brought me back to life!"

I was laughing harder, sure I sounded more than a little hysterical, but Chase humored me with a small grin as he sat tentatively on the edge of the bed.

"Tell me what happened next," I asked through peals of laughter that seemed unlikely to fade soon. "So, I died at the beginning of sophomore year, right? But what about the rest of high school? That was real, right?"

His face darkened. "It was," he said slowly, cautiously. "We loved each other. We went through some shit, but we loved each other."

"Yeah?" I smiled, my gaze falling to my lap. The idea that my memories of him, at least, was a whole truth brought some comfort.

"It's true you were depressed. I was too. But... We could talk about it, at least. And the things we didn't tell other people, we could talk about those too."

I looked at Chase through my lashes, head tilted, faint smile still in place. *Keep going. I need to know.*

"Like," he said, "when you realized you were bisexual and didn't, like, fully understand how you felt, but I still loved you. We went to Pride together in 2020, the cicada year. Remember?"

I nodded eagerly.

"Or when white people would yell at me about eating bat soup in the street, or when men would yell at you about your ass, we were there for each other. They were different struggles, for sure, and a little bit impossible for either of us to entirely understand, but we cared, and that was enough. When something happened to one of us, the other would squeeze their hand, and we would stand just a little bit closer together and feel just a little bit safer."

I remembered that. That was real. Even now, the thought of his hand squeezing mine made me feel warmer, and I wished my hands weren't tied together above me.

"So, why the Gucci belt?" I asked, jerking my head upward and raising my eyes to indicate my bound wrists.

Chase frowned and scooted a little closer to me on the bed. "Right." He sighed. "Umm. So, you started having these dreams, toward the end of high school. We were all set up to flee the East Coast and go to college, ready to celebrate our senior summer, but suddenly it was like your memories were all over the place. You kept talking about a room that looked like an alien spaceship and how cold it was, and you would talk in your sleep. 'She's not me.' 'I'm not her.' That sort of thing. It was kind of creepy. We looked it up, and exorcists are crazy expensive, so we decided to investigate ourselves. One night, we were searching around the hospital, through your dad's lab, and you found this... secret door kind of thing, very sci-fi. You pushed a button in his desk, and half the wall swung around."

"How did we get in his lab?" I wondered. "There's a guard there."

He stared at me, as if waiting for me to realize something. When it was clear I wasn't going to, he sighed. "Ivy, do you remember there ever being a guard in front of your dad's lab growing up?"

"No…" I trailed off, thinking. "My mom has some secretaries, but I think I could beat Anna and Kim in a fight if I had to. Well, maybe not both at once, but I could definitely take them one-on-one."

"Right," he snorted. "Ivy, there's a guard outside your father's lab *because* we broke in last summer."

"Oh." *That made sense.*

"We found those creepy tunnels, and you weren't as familiar with them, so we kept getting lost, but eventually we found that lab, the one you had described. We found some of your dad's notes and started to figure out what had happened and…" He stopped.

I leaned forward, at least, as much as I could with my arms restrained. "And?"

Chase looked at me, leaning forward too, so that our faces were only inches apart. His gaze darted around me, taking in my eyes, which I was sure made me look like a cartoon character, and my mouth, which had fallen slightly ajar.

"Are you sure you're doing okay with all this, Ivy? We can take a break if you need a minute to process anything."

For one stupid moment, my only thought was that I wished he had called me "princess," like he used to. His use of my real name made me feel like a stranger somehow when we were just on the verge of being close again.

"I need to know," I whispered. "I need know my own life."

He nodded, slowly, and moved one hand to gently brush aside a piece of hair I hadn't even noticed was covering my face. "You were already depressed. You always were. Your brain chemistry has been out of whack for as long as I've known you. You didn't get treatment, so you kept spiraling, feeling more hopeless and numb and like you didn't know exactly who you were. This was just the final straw. Learning that you weren't exactly, you know, *you*, pushed you over the edge."

Chase paused, gauging my reaction. He must have deemed my face suitably non-depressed, because he went on.

"You must have realized I would stop you, because you soaked a scrub mask in some anesthetic and held it over my face until I went to sleep. That was why I thought to do it last night with you." He paused. "It was actually really easy to bring you here. I just put my sunglasses on you and told the Uber driver you were drunk. When I brought you back to the hotel they did *not* want to ask questions—one of the perks of being in DC."

I looked around the hotel room again for the first time since I had woken up, realizing it looked familiar. "Are we at the Watergate?"

He gave me an apologetic shrug. "This is where my hotel room was."

"Chase!" I cried, a little too loudly. "You're keeping me hostage at a historical landmark?"

"You know, I want to believe you're talking about the political incident, but—"

"Prom night, Chase! We took each other's virginity at *this* hotel, and this was where you decided to keep me hostage?" I needed to stop yelling, but I couldn't.

He threw up his hands, exasperated. "Do you want to hear the rest of the story or not?"

I rolled my eyes, took a deep breathe, and nodded, trying not to glare.

Chase waited a beat and then kept going.

"You wrote me that note and left your diary open to it next to me. By the time I woke up, you had jumped, and they knew we had been down here. I barely had time to shove your journal in a stack of books before this intense government lady found me and started asking me a million questions."

"You kept the US government from reading my diary?" I almost smiled, my irritation ebbing away.

"What are friends for?" He laughed before his face fell somber again. "They told me you were dead, Ivy. Really dead. They lied and said the project had failed and you were gone and I had better go to California and forget this ever happened or they would have me arrested for espionage. I guess they ran some program that kept us blocked on each others' social media accounts and sent you that stupid text from my phone. I was devastated; it never occurred to me the freaky lady was lying. I went to college. I tried to move on."

You're just not worth it anymore.

I had the sudden, horrible realization that for someone in the government to realize those exact words would convince me Chase had moved on, they must have read through all our texts. They must have seen us repeat those words, over and over again, reassuring each other that we were worth loving, worth all the bad parts just to get the good parts too.

My stomach twisted, and I wondered if I might be sick.

"Why didn't they just, like, erase you from my memory if they thought me knowing about you was so dangerous?"

I could practically see his brain trying to fit the puzzle pieces together. "I don't think it works like that," he finally said slowly. "I think your memories were sort of an all-or-nothing deal. Otherwise, you probably wouldn't have dreams about that lab either."

"They couldn't erase the truth," I murmured, thinking it through. "So, they manipulated it. They gave me half-truths… things that could have been real but weren't." There it was again: the idea that lies held more power when they contained a hint of the truth.

No wonder I had felt like I was going insane.

"You know," Chase said cautiously, "just because you died doesn't mean you can't live a full, happy life. You can—"

I burst out laughing. "Oh my god, Chase. I love you, but you should never become a motivational speaker. You're horrible at it."

He lurched back toward the edge of the bed, as though I had shocked him.

"What?" I asked, confused.

"Nothing," he muttered, "It's just, you said… Never mind."

I didn't quite understand, but I kept going. "It's like you said, though. Learning about this isn't what made me suicidal, it was just the final push. But that stuff comes from, like, brain chemistry and environment, and since last summer I've been going to therapy and taking antidepressants and everything. Aside from the whole psycho-amnesiac thing, my mental health has been pretty good."

"Really?"

I nodded. "Life's not, like, perfect, but it's good. I wish I had figured out how to talk to my parents about things in high school. I was so worried about disappointing them, but I guess more than anything they just wanted me to be okay." I hadn't said those words aloud before, but it felt like I had known for a while. Even when we were distant, even when we didn't understand each other, they loved me, maybe more than any one person deserved to be loved. *Enough to bring me back from the dead, and even the genie from* Aladdin *wouldn't do that.*

I was a little pissed at them for keeping my own death hidden from me, but I kind of understood their decision even if I disagreed with it.

I wondered vaguely what our family dinner would look like when I told them I knew what they had done. Maybe we would fight. Maybe my mom and I would raise our voices at each other while my dad's eyebrows grew more and more pinched together. Maybe someone would cry and someone else would storm out before dessert.

But I knew, inevitably, that we would calm down. We would see eye-to-eye and remember that we loved each other and say as much out loud. We would grasp each other in an awkward, desperate hug, and the fight would pass.

I ran through the list of unexplained things in my mind then as I sat next to Chase. "Okay, so the government convinced me that you had dumped me and didn't want to talk again and convinced you that I was permanently dead. Why did you come to Wollstone then if you didn't know I was alive?"

"To see your parents."

"My parents?" Chase and my parents had never been close.

He looked down at his hands. "I needed closure. I thought it might help."

I still didn't quite understand, but maybe I would have if I had been the one grieving.

I picked out another detail that was bothering me. "You said last time we entered the tunnels through my dad's lab. How did I know they would be on floor K?"

Chase shifted a little and squeezed his eyes shut before he came up with an answer. "I'm not sure," he ventured. "But I think that's the way you left, after you knocked me out. You jumped off the roof, right? Of Witt?"

Oh! Of course. I even remembered that, I realized. I had found the old elevator in the new age tunnels and ridden it to the top. *I had jumped.*

I pursed my lips. "Why... Why is it called 'Pandora'? I don't actually remember that story having anything to do with clones."

"I think your dad probably named it. He's a bit nerdy, right?"

I nodded. I lovingly referred to my father as a nerd all the time. That was one of the only ways you could make fun of someone with an MD *and* a PhD, which, of course, I had to do. Bickering with my parents was part of my required role as the teenage daughter.

"So," continued Chase, "in the story, right, there was a lot of evil and power in a box that ended up with this girl, Pandora. She opened it, and evil and horrible things escaped into the world."

"And?" This girl Pandora sounded kinda dumb. I decided we would have been good friends.

"*And*, even though it sucked the box was opened and had all these bad side effects, at the end of the story the box contained hope."

Hope. That was *exactly* the sort of thing my dad would name his scientific breakthrough. It wasn't a cure for the coronavirus, or my depression, or any of the other things that killed people, and it was sure as hell risky to use, but with that risk came hope. Hope that the world leaders it brought back could do their job and end the pandemic.

Hope that his daughter would heal.

"Are you crying?" asked Chase.

"No." I sniffled.

He nodded, smiling, and leaned over to wipe a tear from my face. His hand was soft and familiar on my cheek, and it lingered just a little longer than it needed to.

We were close, so close together in this bed, and he hadn't deserted me. He had come back for me. Maybe if I kissed him now, everything would go back to the way it was.

I shook my head to clear it. *No. Not yet. Focus.* I had too much to think about right now. It would be stupid to let my hormones take over just as I had finally learned the truth. I needed to reevaluate, to decide what it meant that I wasn't Ivy, that I had died.

"Will you untie me?" I asked softly. "I need to go home."

Chase looked a little disappointed but reached above my head and undid his belt anyway.

"Are you sure you're okay?" he asked.

I nodded. "Just one more question?"

He didn't hesitate. "Anything."

"Do you think I'm her? Ivy, I mean? The girl you…" I couldn't finish the sentence.

He finished freeing my wrists, only to enclose them in a firm grip, pulling me close. "I don't think you're the exact same girl I met in 2020. But," he added quickly, reading the disappointment in my face, "I'm not the same guy I was, either. Maybe we would both be different if you had never died. But maybe we would have been worse. It's not worth wondering who you might have been, who *that girl* might have been if she'd grown up the normal way. It's like wondering what might have happened if you hadn't tripped that day in the street. If we'd never met."

His voice grew softer as his grip on my wrists grew tighter. "*You*," he said. "This version of you, right now, is the girl I fell in love with. The girl who's worth unravelling government conspiracies and cleaning vomit off my shoes. *You.*"

I looked into his dark brown eyes, and they were as warm as the day we had met. And for the first time since I had read that horrible text so many months ago, I really believed him.

CHAPTER THIRTEEN

IF ONLY THE GOOD DIE YOUNG, WHAT DOES THAT MAKE ME?

———

The walk back to Wollstone from the Watergate wasn't that long. I told Chase I needed to walk home alone to clear my head, and he agreed. Well, he agreed after I said that if he didn't, I could call 911 and tell them I was being stalked by an ex-boyfriend. The walk was refreshing, like a little main character moment as I strolled along the Potomac waterfront toward my university, towering on a hill like a Victorian castle.

I realized, in the chilly light of day, that my clothes were wrinkled and a little bit dirty, probably from Chase struggling to maneuver me into an Uber. I'd been wearing spandex and the oversized Wollstone sweatshirt that I'd never actually given back to Will: my official uniform of choice for pulling an all-nighter or for frantically trying to write down every memory I'd ever had until my past made sense. I had been so eager to meet Chase, to go down to floor K and know I wasn't crazy, that I hadn't bothered to change.

As I passed alternating groups of suit-wearing profession-als rushing to meetings and tourists clad fanny packs and "I heart DC" shirts, I noticed a few people looking at me for just a beat too long. A few men ogled my fitted shorts, and a few older people shot me judging stares that I didn't quite understand until I realized, in my rumpled state, I looked like I was on a walk-of-shame.

Oops.

Walking home from being held hostage and learning about my own death was a kind of walk-of-shame, I sup-posed. Still, this wasn't as bad as the time I had accidentally ran into the Secretary of State and her security team, heels in hand, at nine o'clock on a Saturday morning.

I tried to block out all the people from my mind and focus on my newest dilemmas.

Am I a real person?

If I am a real person, is that person Ivy Bell?

If I'm not Ivy Bell, does that mean I need to change my name and do one of those crisis haircuts, where you give your-self bangs in a gas station bathroom?

How would I even begin to figure this out?

On the one hand, I wanted to believe Chase when he said I was the girl he had fallen in love with. I wanted to believe that I was just as much of a human being as that dying fifteen-year-old had been. On the other hand, it seemed dangerous to put my sense of self entirely in the hands of one person, especially if that one person was boy.

So, how could I know? My friends at Wollstone had only ever known this version of me. They had nothing to compare me to, no way to know if I was an entirely different person. My parents, good as their intentions may have been, had already proven that they would lie to me if they thought it was best.

Wait! This was philosophical, right?

Surely trying to figure out whether I was alive was somehow related to the good life, right? Professor Whitby would love this kind of thing, even if I had to phrase it to her as a hypothetical concept for my overdue extra credit paper so she wouldn't think I was crazy.

I could totally frame this as a thought experiment, right? If a person had the exact same DNA as you, and the exact same memories, would that person be you?

I pulled out my phone and typed up a quick email to Professor Whitby, so excited to send it that I barely remembered to remove the "Sent from my iPhone" tag at the bottom.

I had made it less than two blocks closer to Wollstone when her response arrived in my inbox. *"Meet me for office hours in twenty minutes. Second floor of Gotland Hall. In the meantime, google* Ship of Theseus.*"*

The last three words had a link attached, but I was more concerned with the first sentence. *Twenty minutes.* By liberal estimates, I was at least twenty-*five* minutes away; I was a little too short to be fast at the whole walking thing. I really needed to talk to her though… Professor Whitby got *paid* to think about this stuff by a top tier university, so she would have to be able to help, right?

Fuck it, I thought, and I started to run.

***

Forty-five minutes later, I was starting to think that things were not okay.

I had been sitting in the hall outside Professor Whitby's office for over half an hour, staring at the ornate wooden door and collecting judging glances from passing students as they saw my crumpled, desperate state. I had knocked on her door seven times. I had emailed her four more times. I had even checked with the professor next door to make sure I was at the right office. But she was gone. Her office was locked and dark, and she wasn't in it.

So why had she asked me to meet her here?

Why email me back if she was going to disappear?

And what was I supposed to do now? If I ever figured this shit out, I was going to write a guide. *Finding Out You're Un-Dead for Dummies.* It would be a best-seller. I would go on Oprah. *Definitely.*

A notification popped up on my phone, and for a second my heart caught in my chest, sure that it would be Professor Whitby, sure that she was almost here and would help me figure out *everything.*

It was Henley. "*Will I see you tonight??*"

I blinked. Did we have plans? We couldn't. I had barely talked to anyone all week. I fired back two question marks.

"*...The Democracy Ball?*" she responded.

Holy shit, was that tonight? It seemed like ages ago that my mom had helped me find the perfect dress. I had been so excited. I was still excited, right? *Ivy Bell would be excited for this ball,* I told myself. *You are excited for this ball.*

And I was... Mostly...

My phone lit up, another text from Henley. "*You have to come!! I want a dance!*"

I closed my eyes shut, searching for an excuse not to go, but... Why couldn't I? It wasn't like I would be any more dead tomorrow. My quarter life crisis could wait. *Wait. That's not right. Third life crisis? I'll have to figure this out for the manual.*

I turned away from Professor Whitby's office, finally accepting that she wasn't going to come. I would go home. I would take a hot shower. I would get ready for the ball.

***

Campus was buzzing. People were excited for the ball tonight, and they all huddled in colorful clumps of coats and backpacks. They stood out brightly against the trees, which seemed to have finally, truly given up for the year. Not a single leaf remained in the sky, and the ones on the ground looked brown. Dead.

Ha, kind of like me.

As I passed through a courtyard, I gave weak smiles to the people who waved at me; I was too exhausted to try and remember their names or where I knew them from. I could barely even find joy in listening to the snatches of conversation that I usually loved, like individual threads in the tapestry that made up Wollstone's student body.

"It's so fucking cold, I heard it's supposed to snow tonight during the Dem Ball."

"Where's global 'warming' when you need it, huh?" Followed by a frustrated, "We talked about this, Randy: It's climate *change*."

A girl, tall and slim like a model, gushed that she "found the sexiest ballgown! Tonight, I'm totally going to check 'seduce a senator' off my Wollstone bucket list."

"Did you guys have an abacus growing up?"

"No, but I had a gun."

Wait, I knew those last two voices.

"Is that, like, a Southern thing, Harrison?" asked Aiden, and I turned to see my friends clustered together to my left. "Or is there a really interesting part of your childhood that we haven't learned about yet?"

Harrison wrinkled his nose. "It's a Southern thing. I've never shot anything *alive*. I would never!"

"So, no one else had an abacus?" implored Emilia.

"I think you're just a nerd," said Aiden.

"True," I added, walking up to them. "But when you're the CEO of a Fortune 500 company, I will happily live in your pool house."

"Ivy!" cried Will, picking me up and spinning me in a circle.

I giggled, the rush of air on my face feeling wonderful after my crappy night.

Emilia eyed me. "You probably should have made sure she wasn't feeling sick anymore before you twirled her around," she told Will. "I do *not* want to spend the afternoon before the Democracy Ball cleaning up vomit."

I laughed harder, but Will looked worried. "*Are* you feeling better?"

I nodded. "Much."

"Good," said Aiden. "It turns out philosophy isn't as fun when you're not there trying to convince me that 'utilitarianism is the *Pitch Perfect 3* of normative ethical theories.'"

My mouth fell open. "Aiden Ricci!" I gasped. "Did you just publicly admit that I'm a joy to have in class?"

He raised his eyebrows but gave me a small side hug. "Only because you were sick."

"I stand by that theory, you know." I grinned. "*Pitch Perfect 3* tried to appeal to a wider audience by adding mystery, action, and suspense to a series that was already trying to fulfill the categories of 'musical' and 'comedy.' The Bellas' initial performance of 'Toxic' was pretty good, but overall, the film was a watered-down version of the first two and received significantly lower overall ratings because it tried to make *everyone* happy rather than focusing on pleasing just musical comedy fans like in the original—"

"Ivy," Aiden interrupted. "Still not going to watch the movie, still have no idea if you're right or not."

"I'm, like, sixty percent sure that I am."

"Good enough."

The five of us began walking back toward Witt to get ready for the ball.

Maybe it doesn't matter if I'm Ivy, I thought as I walked through my favorite place with four of the people I loved most in the world. *Maybe it doesn't matter precisely who you are so much as it matters that you can love and be loved.*

For one impulsive moment, I almost told them. *Hey guys. I'm dead. Or, at least the first version of me is dead.* I didn't even know how to explain.

Harrison would likely tell me how incredibly sorry he was for what I had gone through and say the sweetest things about how glad he was that I was alive, clone or not. Will would listen patiently as I described every emotion I was feeling in excruciating detail, and then help me come up with a plan to broach the subject to my parents. He would probably even offer to come with me as backup when I did confront them. Aiden would say something like, "Really? This is the third iteration of you, and this is as good as they could do?" But then he would hug me for as long as I needed and make me a big cup of my vanilla tea even though he always claimed he hated the pervasive smell. Emilia would offer to beat up the

US government officials for me. Scratch that, Emilia probably *would* beat up US government officials for me.

The thing was, though, that the reason I knew they would all jump into action to help me was because they had all done it so many times before.

Harrison had once stayed an hour late at a party, just two days after we met, because the girl I had agreed to be "walk-home buddies" with had disappeared. I had been terrified and sobbing that I didn't want to leave her behind, that it wasn't safe, and Harrison stepped up, stayed, and searched until we found her.

Will had once literally carried me home, damsel-in-distress-style, when I had been unable to walk back by myself. Like fucking Superman.

Aiden had been there when I was standing at a party and a boy had wrapped his arms around me, hands on my breasts, his arms so tight that I couldn't move and was too afraid to speak. Aiden had put the fear of God in that boy, not to mention the cold stares he had given cat-callers in the street, stopping them in their tracks.

And Em had always listened, patient as I cried, every time a night ended with something I didn't want to tell the boys about, every time something happened that I knew I would try to forget the next day. She would hold me and tell me it was okay and reassure me that these things happened to other girls too. My boys, for all that I loved them, could never reassure me of *that*.

I heard this analogy once about the oxygen masks you wear on a plane. They always say, in the safety demonstration, that even if you want to help other people with their oxygen masks, you must put your own on first. If you put your own mask on, not only will you have saved yourself, but you'll also have bought yourself time where you're awake and conscious, in which you can continue to help other people. If you try to save everyone else, you'll pass out or maybe die, and then you can't help anyone.

My friends were the type of people who wanted to help everyone else breathe, though sometimes I felt like I was the one who sucked all the oxygen from the room.

I couldn't carry any of them or intimidate someone for them. I felt kind of useless, like all I was doing was asking for help, stealing their oxygen masks.

And here I was, with the biggest emotional burden you could lay on a person, my own literal death, and I was contemplating asking them for help *again*. I couldn't do it.

"Ivy?" asked Emilia, pulling me from my thoughts. We were only a block away from Witt now, and the sight of our home made me feel a little warmer inside.

"Yeah?" I responded, plastering on the brightest smile I could.

"We're listing the most out-there songs we have on a sex playlist," filled in Will.

I pursed my lips. "I feel like…" I looked at Em. "I feel like you would think it was one of the Taylor Swift songs."

"*No!*" Emilia gasped. "Please tell me you do not have Taylor Swift songs on a sex playlist."

"Not, like, her country stuff," I clarified.

Aiden was squinting at me, his mouth twisted in horror. "There's *no* acceptable Taylor Swift song to have on a sex playlist."

"Not even 'Wildest Dreams'?"

Even Harrison was emphatically shaking his head at me.

"I have 'I Kissed a Girl' on one of them, but it's a playlist I only use if I'm actually with a girl, if that helps," I said, giggling.

"I don't think I can live with you anymore," Emilia declared.

"Well, what do you have? Billy Joel? 'Scenes from an Italian Restaurant'?" I asked.

"First of all," Em paused a beat to make sure I was listening, "no, I do not have Billy Joel songs on my sex playlist. I have sexy songs, like every other human being in the world."

"'Wildest Dreams' is se—"

"Second of all," she continued, briefly pulling out her Wollstone student ID and scanning it at the security pad as we reached the door of Witt, "you can't even *name* ten Billy Joel songs, so don't talk to me."

"I *so* can!" I retorted.

"By the time we get back to our room?" Will asked as we passed the security guard. "We can bet on the next round of coffee at Company."

I paused, deciding. "Okay."

"I'm team Emilia," Aiden said quickly.

"Same," added Will.

Harrison glanced between us. "I'll take Ivy."

Emilia and I shook, just as we reached the elevators. She leaned over to push the "up" button.

"Wait!" I threw my hand out to stop her. "We should take the stairs," I said with a wicked grin. "Seeing as I'm all traumatized and all."

Will, Aiden, and Emilia groaned, but Harrison gave me a subtle fist bump.

***

Twenty minutes later the five of us were in room 603, sprawled about in various states of preparing for the ball even though it wasn't for another six hours. At this point we were solidly in the "eating snacks," "petting Whiskey," and "pre-ball nap" stages of our preparation. Aiden was still grumbling occasionally that I had forced us to climb seven flights of stairs and still had only named nine Billy Joel songs, to which I replied that I was pretty sure "Walking in Memphis" really was by Billy Joel, and we should probably check again just to be sure.

I grabbed my pink towel, fluffy bathrobe, and shower caddy and headed to the sixth floor girls' bathroom. It was early enough in the afternoon that it was blissfully empty, so I hopped in the good shower, the one where the water got hot and there was barely any hair stuck to the wall. I took full advantage of the solitude and turned up the volume on my phone as loud as it went, singing along to "Gold Rush" by Taylor Swift.

I took the longest shower of my life. I put coconut oil in my hair before washing it to make it soft. I exfoliated my entire body. I shaved *everything*. I used my fanciest vanilla-glitter body wash. I smoothed my feet with a pumice stone. I moisturized every inch of my body. Twice.

I did every self-care thing I could possibly think of, and it only took an hour. *Fuck.*

By the time I made it back to our room, wrapped in my robe with my hair piled high up in a towel, everyone else was asleep, Emilia and Aiden in her bed, Harrison and Will in mine. I tried to move quietly around the room, because even though Emilia could sleep through a nuclear detonation, I was sure the boys couldn't.

I went methodically through a list of self-care tasks, trying to force myself to feel grounded in my body. I painted my nails a soft pink that would go perfectly with my dress. I dried and curled my hair until it fell in little princess waves. I began to do my makeup and couldn't help but feel extra focused on the way my features looked.

My eyes were nice, colored a sparkly blue, and I had lashes that had been gathering compliments since the fourth grade. I always accentuated them with as bold of an eyeliner I felt I could pull off for a given event. For the Democracy Ball, I gave them a round look, like a cartoon princess, with perfect wings branching off the sides. I liked the way my nose looked from the front, but I hated my side profile. It felt just a little too angular. I used contour and highlight to make it just a bit more subtle. My lips were small, but I had long since given up trying to make them look bigger with liner. It always looked fake in the end, so I simply swiped on a lipstick in the same pale pink as my nails.

As I stared at my face, I wondered if anyone had thought about changing me at all the second or third time around. That was stupid. Of course my parents wouldn't do that, but I couldn't help myself from imagining a slightly different girl, Ivy Bell if she had just one strand of different DNA.

Maybe I would be taller and I wouldn't dislike my legs so much. Or maybe I would have a better attention span and I would be acing all my classes right now. *Hmm.*

Whiskey squeaked behind me, and I grabbed him one of the fancy rat treats that Harrison had gifted me from the farmers market. He squeaked, and I smiled.

***

"Your makeup looks amazing," Emilia gushed a few hours later, when my friends had finally woken up and we were finishing getting dressed, dancing around to our group's joint playlist.

I grinned and pulled on my dress. It was emerald green silk, the best I had ever worn. The top was tight with a V-neck and spaghetti straps. It made my boobs look so good that I felt like a modern-day Helen of Troy; I could send two fraternities to war. The skirt was long and full, the kind that puffs up when you spin, which of course Will and I immediately did. It was the perfect dress, even before you factored in that it had pockets.

I felt beautiful for one minute. I really did. I looked at my reflection and saw a girl in a pretty dress getting ready for a party with her friends. She was beautiful. She was alive.

But then I looked down at my phone, and I saw a text from Henley. *"I'll be in a red dress ;)."*

And I was suddenly miserable, because I wasn't entirely sure that girls who had died were still allowed to fall in love.

"Ivy, are you crying?" Emilia whispered softly so that the boys couldn't hear her over the music. "Are you okay?"

She was wearing a black satin jumpsuit that she had sewn herself. Her face looked perfect, airbrushed, like she had just walked out of a black and white film.

Well, almost perfect.

"Let me fix your eyeliner," I said, trying to keep my voice steady and light, trying to force myself back into the lighter mood I'd been in just a minute ago. "The wing's a mess."

"Then let it be messy," she said. "What's really going on? For better or for worse, you are the type of person who talks about your problems, usually to the point of oversharing. So, what's different about this one? What can't you tell me?"

I blinked back my tears—in two blinks, which was probably a world record—and asked, "Do you think we would
still be friends if we weren't roommates? Like, if we just met
each other on the street or something? Do you think we still
would have loved each other?"

"No," she said after a moment of thought. "I don't think
we would have. But that doesn't matter right now. What's
going on, like in our timeline?"

"It's nothing," I said, turning away. She was probably
right. The real Ivy wouldn't have been friends with Emilia,
or the boys, or anyone here. The real Ivy wouldn't have had
any of them, any of this. This life wasn't real. I wasn't real.
I was dead.

That was what the last girl had thought, the second girl,
whoever she was. She had realized that she was dead and that
she was supposed to be dead. She had decided to make it a
reality. And maybe, just maybe, she was right.

CHAPTER FOURTEEN

IF I HAD JUST FLIRTED WITH SOME DIPLOMATS, I WOULDN'T BE ABOUT TO DIE

———

When our Uber dropped Will, Emilia, Aiden, Harrison, Rose, and me off at the ball, the sun had begun to set, and the grounds of Ryland Manor were painted in a delicate golden light. Ryland, the ball's venue, was an old mansion just outside the district that had been lovingly designed by a famous architect as a gift for his wife. It looked hauntingly beautiful now, in the fading glow of the day.

Brick paths wandered lazily around imposing statues and bubbling fountains before they reached a huge maze of tall hedges, the entrance just barely illuminated and covered in a dense carpet of leaves. Even the elaborate gardens still looked beautiful in the late November chill, with their thick bushes full of red berries and a few of the flowering plants still stubbornly holding on to their petals.

Groups of people strolled up the path toward massive front doors, radiating the sounds of laughter and swooshing skirts on stone as they went. Hundreds of windows lined the walls, framing moments of revelry behind glass panes like living portraits of the delighted guests.

I stumbled slightly on my emerald skirt, awestruck by the beauty of it all and unable to focus totally on the task of stepping out of the car. Will caught me before I hit the ground.

"Are you sure you're okay?" he whispered.

I nodded, sure my voice would tremble if I tried to actually speak. I was growing more emotional by the minute, unable to quite process what I was feeling or why I was feeling it right now.

A memory floated to the surface of my mind. I was about six or seven, and my dad had shown me how to hook an emergency rope ladder to the sill of my second-story bedroom window. It was part of his fire safety lecture, a way to escape our apartment if a blaze prevented me from using my bedroom door.

"You have to remember to stay calm," he had said. "Do as much as you're able to get out by yourself, and I'll come to help you as soon as I can."

"That doesn't make any sense," I protested. "If the fire's blocking my door, and I can't get out, how would you be able to get in?" I remembered shaking my little head stubbornly, sure he was confused.

"It does make sense," he argued calmly back, "because I'm your dad. Best case scenario, it's better for me to get just a few burns getting over there than for you to get a lot of burns trying to leave. Worst case scenario,"—and despite all of the memories my mind had lost over the years, I had never quite managed to forget the unwavering look on his face—"you have a lot more of your life left to live than I do. I'd do anything to make sure you get the chance to be there for it."

Now, as I stood together with my closest friends taking in one of the most wonderful sights I had ever seen and about to begin what I was sure would be one of the best nights of my life, I felt tears stinging in the corners of my eyes. Even at the age of seven, I had felt how much he truly meant those words, and I knew now he had never stopped meaning them, either.

I was sure that if my dad could have given himself the coronavirus three years ago instead of me, he would have. Instead, he had been forced to save me the only way he knew how: using the science and medicine he had devoted his life to studying.

I had a father who had changed the known laws of science and a mother who had negotiated millions of dollars on a top-secret project with the federal government, all because they loved me. All because they wanted me to live, for me to experience moments like this.

Despite every horrible thought my depressed mind had ever thrown at me and every thought that might come in the future as I continued to heal, in that moment I felt like the luckiest and most loved girl in the entire world.

***

Inside the house, the party was just as perfect. Chandeliers hung from high ceilings, dripping with crystals and warm candlelight. Colorful dresses and crisply pressed suits wove in easy movements around the room, carrying with them my classmates and professors, public figures, and famous Wollstone alumni. It might have looked like something out of a Jane Austen book if not for the more revealing dresses and the Xray machines that had been set up near the entrance as part of a thorough security check.

"May I have this dance?" Harrison asked Rose with a sweet bow of his head, while Will said, "I'm going to go get us drinks at the bar."

"Wait!" I blurted, just a little too loudly for the room. "We need to get a picture first."

"Didn't you already take pictures at Witt?" protested Aiden.

"No, I took, like, three selfies. That totally doesn't count. We need a picture of us here, at the dance!" I leaned against him pleadingly. "What if you want to make a scrapbook someday?"

He raised an eyebrow. "Do you really think I'm going to make a scrapbook someday?"

"You totally are," Rose interjected, and without giving him a chance to reply she found a nice-looking girl standing near us in the crowd and asked her to take our photo.

We gathered in a line near the edge of the room so that we wouldn't be in the way of all the moving party guests. Rose and Harrison were at the end, pressed together in an embrace. Will had one arm around them and one on me, with Emilia and then Aiden following.

One photograph later, I was pressed against Will's side and my other arm was holding Em tightly by the waist. Her head was on my shoulder, and Aiden was leaning down, reaching across us too.

Three photographs later, we had dissolved into a messy group hug with tangled arms pulling each other tightly into the fold. No one was quite looking at the camera, and my face was pressed in a smile so wide that my cheeks began to burn. It was perfect.

After that, we began to break up and explore the various levels of the house. I saw Harrison spinning Rose on the dance floor as Em and I walked up a wooden staircase, lightly sipping on mojitos.

"I heard," she was telling me, "that the president is supposed to come tonight. That's why the security was so intense."

"The president of the university?" I asked, confused.

She rolled her eyes. "No, Ivy, the president of *America*. Hillmore!"

Oh. Thoughts clicked into place. I realized the men in suits performing the security check at the door really *had* looked like Secret Service agents, and I had just been too caught up in my own death to notice. Then I remembered a slightly more disturbing fact.

President Hillmore died three years ago.

Emilia was looking at me, waiting for a reaction. "So?"

"So..."

"Don't you want a picture with him? This is the perfect time; you look really hot!" She tugged gently on one of my blonde curls for emphasis.

Right. Em already had pictures with the president, and I could vaguely remember joking about it once, saying I wanted a picture too to even the score. She had remembered and was trying to make sure I got one. I thought my heart might melt.

"We should totally get one together with him if we see him!" I said and prayed we wouldn't. I didn't think I could handle getting that close to a man who had literally died, especially the Commander in Chief. I was already feeling loopy from dealing with my own existential crisis. I didn't want to think about America's existential crisis too. "In the meantime, let's aim for mingling with slightly lower-level officials, like a senator or an ambassador. I bet there's *totally* some cute ambassadors."

Em grinned. "Just don't flirt with any Secret Service agents. Don't go anywhere *near* a Secret Service agent. I don't want to get arrested before I even have a green card."

"Hmm…" I wiggled my eyebrows playfully. "Maybe someone here is ordained! We could get married, you could have dual American-Argentine status, and *then* we can get arrested."

"Not even *close* to how that works, Ivy," said Emilia, laughing.

"Okay, okay," I conceded. "Not tonight." I took a long, deliberate drink from my mojito before adding, "That will just give us something to look forward to for the future, then." Em laughed again before our attention was diverted by a passing waiter with a tray of hors d'oeuvres.

I took a spear of gruyere and prosciutto and wrapped it in a napkin before slipping it into my pocket to bring home to Whiskey. Both foods were on the list I had been accumulating of internet-approved treats that were safe for rats. I also wanted the lavish stick the snack was served on, which was made of polished brown wood and shaped like a miniature sword with Wollstone's school seal stamped on the handle. Wicked cool.

I was starting to understand how this ball inspired so many alumni donations. Our school had gone all out, and I was sure that even the billionaires were impressed.

After we finished exploring the different floors of the mansion, Emilia and I found Will and Aiden and ended up back in the main room. Dancing people filled it now, moving slowly and formally through the room. It was funny to think that these were the same students I had seen drunkenly bouncing to horrible pop music on dozens of occasions. Wollstone looked elegant tonight. *I look elegant tonight*, I thought as I caught my reflection in a large, gilded mirror on the opposite wall. My hair hung down in a waterfall of blonde perfection, my dress hugged my body perfectly with the green silk of the skirt billowing out like in a commercial, and my makeup was just the way I liked it: glittery as hell.

I looked at the public figures in the room too, the congressmen and visiting royalty, many of whom had once gone to Wollstone themselves. I had always seen people like that around campus, prestigious and powerful, looking exactly like they belonged. I thought of all the times I had compared myself to them, the way they seemed to glide on the same brick sidewalks that always made me trip.

Maybe they were like me once. Maybe they used to feel clumsy too, uncertain they were good enough. Maybe they dressed up and started playing a part too, just like we did tonight.

I stared at a man a few feet away whom I vaguely recognized as a former Secretary of Defense. I imagined him in a Wollstone debate T-shirt or arriving on campus as a freshman. I erased the hardened look in his eyes, the wrinkles from his forehead, and pictured a face that was young and vulnerable instead.

I had always believed that for every mark you made on Wollstone, Wollstone made a mark on you. For every brick in the path I had the audacity to wear down with my footsteps, I was given a scuffed boot or skinned knee in return. Maybe I had been wrong. Maybe I had been given something else too.

I looked back to the girl in the gilded mirror. She didn't look exactly like the Ivy Bell of 2020, but she didn't look exactly like the girl who had stared at me back in the psych ward this summer, either. There were changes, subtle changes I hadn't even noticed at the time, but they were there. I hadn't grown, but I stood a little taller now. My posture seemed almost confident, and my chin was held up, just a centimeter to the sky.

I had fallen down hundreds of times, but I had always gotten back up again. I had torn dresses at parties, and Emilia had helped me sew them together again until I understood how to fix them by myself. I had lost my mind, and then I had found it again.

I was not the smartest student at Wollstone, and I would certainly never be the most powerful. I was sure that one day one of my classmates, or a boy I bumped into at a party, or maybe even Henley, would be our new president. I was just as sure that my life would have meaning too.

I turned to Emilia. "What did you mean before," I asked, "when you said you didn't think we would be friends if we weren't roommates?"

Her eyebrows knitted together. "I really don't understand why it matters. I just…" She trailed off.

"Please?" I asked, and she sighed.

"When I first met you, you were all pink and sparkly and blonde and Taylor Swift, and I *might* have told my friends that I thought my new roommate was really basic."

I giggled, remembering the first day we had met after randomly being assigned as roommates. "And now?"

"You're *still* all those things. But now, the pink and the sparkles—they're part of this way bigger picture. They fit in with your personality, and the fact that we have to stop to pet every dog you see on the street, and with all these memories that I love. I'm so glad we're roommates, Ivy. And maybe, *if* we weren't, we wouldn't be friends. Maybe I wouldn't be friends with the boys, either. But we do, and I'm so happy that we do, and I don't want to think that any of the rest of it matters. I—are you *crying*?"

"No!" I sobbed, tears spilling down my face.

"Ivy!" Emilia pulled me into a hug.

"Are you guys okay?" asked Aiden, turning from where he and Will had been chatting together. "Ivy, you've been crying a lot today."

"I'm on my period!" I said, and he nodded vigorously, trying to act supportive even as the color faded in his face.

"Got it. Do you… need anything?"

I was about to say "no" when I spotted a flash of red lace moving toward us across the room.

"I need some air," I responded instead. "I'm going to go walk out in the garden."

"Do you want us to come with?" Will asked.

"No thanks. I'll only be a few minutes, I swear."

"It's supposed to start snowing soon," Em warned. "Don't get hypothermia."

I agreed before darting toward the mansion's back doors toward the grounds. Despite my heels, I moved quickly, rushing to circumvent the girl in the red dress.

Just because I'm not going to avoid all my problems doesn't mean I have to deal with all of them tonight. Right?

Outside, the crowd was thinner. It seemed most of the guests had been deterred by the sharp cold of the night. I saw a couple kissing near a hibernating rose bush and two boys holding hands in a gazebo to my right. I moved past them all, barely remembering to hold up my skirt to prevent the bottom from getting dirty.

I walked away from the few remaining people, toward the labyrinth of hedges. I passed underneath its entrance and found myself a small clearing with an elaborate fountain at the center. The water had been turned off for the year, but the stone itself still looked beautiful, and I wanted to see it up close before I noticed it was already occupied by several men in suits.

"Oh!" I blurted, stumbling backward a step, but it was too late. They had seen me. "I'm so sorry," I stuttered, genuinely nervous now, because the men closest to me were dressed exactly like the Secret Service agents that had let me in at the door.

Oh no. The man in the middle was—

"No, please stay! You just can't tell the First Lady that I came out here to smoke."

It was President Hillmore. *Fuck.*

My frightened gaze darted between his guards, waiting for one of them to contradict him and say that I looked dangerous and should leave. They didn't. *Double fuck.*

The president of the United States was squinting at me now, trying to make out my face in the dregs of light shining out from Ryland Manor. "I'm quite sorry, dear. You look familiar, but… It's dark, and I can't seem to place your name." He frowned, and I got the sense that, unlike me, he was not a person who frequently forgot names.

The horrible thing was, I felt it too. I could *almost* blame my lingering sense that I knew him on his fame, the fact that everyone in the world knew what Collin Hillmore looked like. But it felt deeper than that. Weirder. Like coming across a toy that you had loved as a child but hadn't actually seen in years.

"My name is Ivy, sir," I said nervously. I thought about giving a fake name, but despite any jokes, I really didn't want to be arrested by the Secret Service.

"Collin," he responded, holding out the hand that wasn't clutching a cigarette. "Very nice to see you. Are you a Wollstone student?"

"Yes... I'm a freshman." I cautiously took his hand. His grip was firm, and his handshake felt important, as though I were a foreign head of state at a trade negotiation and not a teenager standing inside a glorified bush.

"Well, Ivy," Hillmore said, and he flashed me a perfect, confident smile. "I bet that you're about to have the best four years of your life."

I nodded, unable to think of anything to say. Despite his cheerful demeanor, I could sense the words had been a dismissal. I thought I uneased him a little, in the same way he uneased me. *Except he doesn't know we both died.*

I walked slowly past the fountain, out of the clearing, and then began to hurry further through the hedges. I didn't look where I was going or concentrate on which turns to take. I kept moving, putting space between us, until I tripped on an uneven patch of dirt and landed sprawled on the ground.

I really, *really* needed to talk to my parents. I wanted to hear about Pandora from them, to hear them explain why they had done it.

Still, I didn't get up. How could I? Even if I left, right now, and found them tonight, what could I possibly say?

Maybe life would be better if I stayed here, until the hedges enveloped me and I was part of Ryland Manor too. That had to be a nice life, right? At least there would be no Russian homework.

"Ivy?"

I jolted and turned to see the swatches of red lace I had come to the grounds specifically to avoid.

"Hey, Henley. How did you find me here?"

Despite the darkness of the night, Henley seemed to burn. Her black hair was pulled in an elaborate updo, held together with a dozen beautiful gold barrettes that looked like tiny sparks. Her dress was strapless and lace, form fitting with a slit in the skirt that reached almost to her left thigh.

"Will showed me. You have that location app on your phone, and he saw you had stopped in this maze, so I looked and found a shortcut to reach you."

Right. I always forgot the phone.

"What happened with you?" Henley asked. "You acted kind of strange at the end of that Halloween party, and then you left by yourself, and you disappeared for, like, a week. I tried to get your attention inside, but… What happened?"

And there it was, the exact question I had been running from. Because honestly, I wanted to tell her. I wanted to tell everyone, but I *really* wanted to tell her. I wanted to unload my problems, to share the ridiculousness of this secret, to talk it over until we forced it to make sense.

Telling Henley was no better than telling my friends: it would just mean burdening her and sounding crazy for no reason. But when she said, "Ivy?" again, in the gentlest voice I could imagine, when she took my hand in hers and asked, "What's wrong?"

I broke.

"So many things are wrong," I said, a little hysterically. "Not irreparably, I think, but my life is insane, and I really want to be okay. I keep thinking of reasons why everything should be okay, but I still feel *overwhelmed*." I was squeezing her hand back, probably a little too tightly, but no matter how many times I tried I couldn't seem to loosen my grip.

Henley's eyes were wide, but she wasn't trying to run away or get me to shut up. That was a good start.

"Tell me what happened," she said.

And I found myself, against all better judgment, telling Henley Gara, "Three years ago, during the pandemic, I got the coronavirus. And I didn't get better."

I started talking in an uncontrollable rush, and as I talked, she pulled me up and we moved further into the maze together. Henley and I walked, hand in hand, away from the party and the rest of our school. Away from everyone and everything. We let the hedges block out all the light.

Henley listened to my story quietly, only interrupting on occasion to ask a clarifying question, until I got to the part where Chase drugged me and tied me up in a hotel.

"He did *what*? I'm going to destroy him. That's so creepy!" she yelled, and honest to God, I smiled. She was so passionate, and it kind of felt wonderful to have someone get worked up like that on my behalf.

"I want to hate him," I said. "I really do. I was hating him for months, but... I don't know, I just keep putting myself in his shoes, and it kind of makes sense."

I could see that world, the world if Chase and I had switched places. I imagined sitting beside a sixteen-year-old Chase, still scrawny and unsure of himself, while he lay bedridden with the virus. We had been so young then, even though it hadn't felt that way at the time. I thought of getting him back months later when he had finally recovered and how overprotective I would feel of him.

If that Chase had started having strange visions in high school, I would have investigated them. I know I would have. And if that Chase had discovered the truth, and killed himself? It would have killed me too. I would have gone to Vanderbilt, would have tried to move on and forget, but I would spend the rest of my life feeling powerless. Chase would always be there in the back of my mind, until one day I couldn't keep him there anymore. And, if I had realized he was still alive, I would have done absolutely anything to get him back.

"Hmm," muttered Henley, and I could tell she didn't agree but was wise enough not to press the issue right now. There were bigger problems.

"Do you really believe me?" I asked, pressing closer to her for warmth.

"Why wouldn't I?"

I snorted. "Well, for one thing, I can barely believe it myself, and I saw all the evidence firsthand."

"You're too close to the situation, though," Henley responded, her voice as calm as if she were explaining a homework assignment. "From the outside, it kind of makes sense. The basic technology for cloning has been around for years, and I think everyone always assumed there was more advancement going on somewhere behind closed doors. And you were right before: 2020 was a shitshow. It was kind of the perfect storm for something like this. Everyone was desperate, materials were running low, and supervision flew out the window in a lot of cases. I mean, I'm sure the government would have been happy just to get back a healthy president, even if they didn't understand exactly how it happened."

"How right you are," came a voice from the darkness on the path up ahead.

I screamed. Loudly. Honestly, I expected glass would shatter at the sound.

Henley only jumped a little, and her voice barely shook as she asked, "Who are you? Who's there?"

A figure stepped forward, and a flashlight came on, and I screamed again.

"I know you're not the smartest girl, Ivy, but really, even you must know that no one can hear you scream from all the way out here."

It was Dr. Thana.

Only, she didn't look like Dr. Thana, not exactly. Her lab coat had been replaced by a sleek black jacket. She had switched her trademark messy bun for a smooth, tight ponytail. Her glasses were gone, and she had done her makeup differently so that she looked younger, more threatening.

Oh, and instead of a clipboard, she was holding a gun.

"What the fuck are you doing here, Dr. Thana?" I asked, more loudly than I had intended to.

"I'm responding to an email," said my presumably ex-therapist. Then, she fired the gun.

Instincts took over, and I pulled Henley to the side as I saw, in quick flashes like stop motion, the bullet whiz just past us. *No. Not a bullet. A dart.*

Why was my therapist trying to shoot me with a dart gun?

My train of thought broke as Henley screamed, "Run!" and began pulling me along back through the maze. We dashed through various turns and tunnels, stumbling on loose roots and holes, holding up our dangling skirts. I was beginning to wish I had worn a jumpsuit tonight, like Serena.

I could hear Dr. Thana behind us, but she hadn't caught up yet. She must have known it would be harder to get us without the darts, as one of us might run away while she fought the other. She sent occasional darts past us, constantly trying for a clean shot.

I just hoped she wouldn't get one.

"Do you know why she is shooting at us?" Henley yelled over sound of our crashing through the trees. Her legs were shorter than mine, and she kept nearly tripping as she ran faster to keep up. I vaguely realized that running through a dark maze in a ballgown and heels was the first thing I had seen Henley Gara do that she wasn't immediately good at.

Huh. I guess everyone has at least one thing, I thought and laughed out loud.

"Why are you laughing?" she cried.

"Because this is ridiculous!" I shouted back, and then she was laughing too.

We were running, laughing, and just turning down a leafy corridor with light at the end of it when Henley went down. Hard.

"Henley!" I screamed, diving to the ground after her.

She was lying, face down in the dirt, a dart sticking out of her back. I pulled it out as quickly as I could, but it was too late. She was already fading, slipping into unconsciousness.

"Henley!" I screamed again. Her eyes were half closed, and she moaned softly.

Oh god, I have to save her. I stuck my arms under hers and began to pull. I dragged her, desperate, slowly toward the entrance and toward the light.

"Just give up, Ivy," said Dr. Thana, suddenly appearing. "You have to know you're not getting away right now."

I ignored her and kept tugging Henley, inch by inch, out of the maze. We were so close, so close I could almost hear the party in the distance.

Dr. Thana walked lazily forward, in no rush to catch up. "Come on, Ivy. This is pointless. Just like you."

I tried to tune her out completely, to see only Henley, to focus on keeping her safe. We were just at the exit now, and if I could just keep going...

Ouch.

I looked down and saw a dart protruding from my arm. I plucked it out with one hand, and kept my other arm wrapped around Henley, pulling her toward the sounds of the people. We were in grass now, soft grass. She should have been easier to pull, only, she wasn't. She felt heavier, so heavy. Or maybe I was feeling weaker.

I looked at Dr. Thana, who was only a few feet away now, leisurely twirling her dart gun around her index finger.

"You know, Ivy," she said, her tone still infuriatingly casual, "this is all *your* fault. If you weren't such an obnoxious little shitbag, then Henley would be perfectly fine right now. Instead…" She *tsked*, like a disappointed preschool teacher. "Well, I don't want to promise anything too soon. All I'll say is, what happens next is on you."

I couldn't stay upright anymore, and I toppled, landing in the grass next to Henley. Green silk spilled onto red lace, and I reached out my hand slowly, painfully slowly, toward hers.

As my eyes began to drift shut, Dr. Thana came into view, standing over us and shaking her head.

"Teenage hormones," she muttered. "They'll ruin everything, every time."

With my last ounce of willpower, I laced my fingers into Henley's. I felt a cold prick on my skin and thought briefly that Dr. Thana had decided to inject me with something else, before a second cold prick came and I realized what it was.

It had finally started to snow.

CHAPTER FIFTEEN

IF I SURVIVE THIS—

———

For the second day in a row, I woke up from a dreamless sleep. It would have been lovely had I not opened my eyes to find I was cuffed to a steel table in a windowless room.

Shit.

Cool metal bands were wrapped around my wrists, ankles, neck, and waist, restraining me from examining my surroundings too closely, but I was pretty sure the room had to belong to the same network of tunnels as that horrible laboratory. It had the same feel of frozen air and harsh fluorescent lighting. I wondered briefly whether it was federal income taxes or someone's hospital bill that had been spent on custom ordering the ten-billion-watt lightbulbs they must use down here.

To shield my eyes from the light, I turned my head as far as I could to the left. Henley laid parallel to me, still unconscious, her dark hair spilling over the side of the table and a few golden pins scattered haphazardly where they must have fallen from her head.

Instinctively, I tried to move to help her, only to choke as my throat jammed into hard steel.

"And here I thought you were going to sleep forever," came a disgusted voice from somewhere across the room. "College students can be so inconvenient that way."

Dr. Motherfucking Thana.

It sounded like she was somewhere beyond my feet, but I couldn't quite see her. *Am I... not wearing any shoes? Where did they go? Wait—that's not important.*

"What's your fucking problem?" I asked hysterically.

I heard angry, rapid typing, and then a mechanical *whir.* The metal behind me began to tilt upward like a dentist's chair might at the end of a routine cleaning, until I was about thirty above horizontal and could make out slightly more of the room. A small metal edge had protruded beneath my feet, preventing me from sliding downward on my silk dress.

Dr. Thana came into view near a massive computer on a desk near the opposite wall. She seemed... *glossy*, down here in this horrible place. Her makeup had been perfectly painted to make her pale skin seem icy instead of sallow, and her red hair still in that same sleek ponytail from the woods. *Did she not even break a sweat chasing us down? That bitch!*

She was wearing a fitted black sweater with black leggings and a tiny leather holster stuck the side of her waist. She had a different gun there now, more solid looking. *How many guns can one person possibly need?* I wondered, purposely ignoring the obvious implication that this gun shot something besides tranquilizer darts.

"Why did you bring me here?" I demanded, trying to ignore the fact I was actively trembling. "Is it fucking kidnap-Ivy-week or something?"

"You know, there have been a lot of academic studies that examine excessive swearing. Some of them seem to differ in their findings connecting curse words to..." Dr. Thana glanced at me, wrinkling her nose, "intelligence… But I have read some interesting theories about profanity as a pain response. I find myself supporting ideas that patients swear when they're exhibiting their fight-or-flight response, when they've lost self-control."

"Don't say *patient*," I spat. "You're not a real doctor."

She narrowed her eyes. "Incorrect, Ivy. I have a doctoral degree from Notre Dame. How very anti-feminist of you to assume I'm uneducated."

"You're insane," said Henley hoarsely from my left, and I tried to turn toward her again.

"I am *not* insane, Ms. Gara. What a rude thing to say." Thana scoffed, and she began typing again. There was the tiniest high-pitched noise, and I saw Henley go limp in my peripheral vision.

I laughed only because I had no idea of what reaction I *should* have. "What is your fucking problem?"

"Entitled *teenagers* who threaten western *stability* are my problem, *Ivy*." She was sneering now, over-enunciating each word. It seemed strange now that I had always thought her so emotionless. "I'm tying up loose ends," she continued. "Like I should have done last summer. Like I would have done if it weren't for your ridiculously inconvenient parents."

"Last summer?"

"Last summer," Thana glared, "a stupid teenage girl and her stupid teenage *feelings* put the security and order of the entire globe at stake. *I* suggested we eliminate the problem, and I was overruled. Some very shortsighted people didn't think that getting rid of *you* was worth losing your parents and their research as a cooperative asset. But that's the government for you, isn't it? Too many people, not enough braincells."

"I don't understand," I protested. Maybe she really was insane. I tried pulling against the cuffs that were restraining me, looking hopelessly for a way out.

"Of course, you don't understand. You're an idiot. You're a stupid, self-centered, naive little girl who would have been gone a long time ago if natural selection still had any say in the matter." Thana sauntered over toward me, her shoes clacking loudly on the white tile. The look in her eye was... inhuman somehow. No... It was more like she didn't think *I* was human, like I was a rabid bat that had invaded her house and she was about to dispose of me.

"Do you have any idea," she continued, "how annoying it was pretending to be your therapist?"

Okay. That hurt.

"I'm a CIA operative, not a preschool teacher. I shouldn't have to listen to the complaints of whiny children," she added with a glare.

"Then why do it?" I asked, and I would have thrown my hands up in exasperation if I hadn't been, well, strapped to a table. "If you really work for the government, why waste your time on me?"

"Because," Thana shouted, "I was the only one willing to step up! I was the only one smart enough to see the risk you posed, the only one responsible enough to take care of it! Three years ago, when your parents asked for permission to use Pandora to bring you back to life, after it had already been used on the president and half a dozen other political assets, *I* knew that wasting that same technology on an over-privileged fifteen-year-old could mean exposing and destabilizing everything Pandora was supposed to protect. Our institutions, our very way of life, were thrown into chaos during that pandemic. The stability of the US was in a delicate, high-risk state, and if we had lost our leaders to the virus and tried to replace them before the next election, it would have led to outcry, claims of illegitimacy, maybe even revolution. And if that secret got out now…"

I tried then, I really did, to see it from her perspective. I had been too young to vote for President Hillmore, but I probably would have if I was able. His opponent had been so outwardly racist and misogynistic, had blamed minorities for the virus and told his followers he was our real leader even after he lost the election, capitalizing on their fear of the pandemic and other people. There had been mobs in the capital after Hillmore won, even when he did it in a regularly scheduled election. I didn't really want to imagine what those mobs might have done if Hillmore had died in office and the change of power had been even more irregular. Surely the nation wouldn't have *actually* self-destructed though, right?

"So, you thought if I were brought back to life in 2020, I might tell someone what had really happened?" I asked, and it took all my confidence to look her in the eyes.

"Can you imagine what would have happened? We've been protecting the balance of world power for years, and the reason we've been so successful is because we exterminate even the smallest potential risks to classified data, especially when we're using methods people might not understand. You saw what happened in Havana seven years ago, where there were only *hints* of esoteric weapon use, and that became international news."

Henley moaned something next to me, but I couldn't understand it. I wanted so badly to reach out and hold her hand.

"How could I have ruined your secret?" I asked, trying to capture Thana's attention before she hurt Henley again. "I didn't even know."

She frowned. "We forbid your parents from telling you. That was part of the deal they agreed to, in exchange for your life. That was why I didn't intervene the first time, even though I probably should have. But you started to remember. We had tried to limit what you saw during the transition, supplemented with scopolamine treatments to control what we could... But something went wrong. You found your way back here, freaked out, and jumped off the roof." Thana sighed and shook her head. "If it were up to me, it would have ended there, but your parents wanted another deal. Another daughter."

"And you actually agreed?"

My ex-therapist rolled her eyes. "I'm not a god, Ivy. I can't just *decide* whether or not to bring someone back from the dead. This is the *United States government*; we have a committee for that."

I heard a strained laugh from my right side. *My right side?* I struggled, forcing my head to turn, millimeter by painful millimeter, toward the sound. There was another steel table there. Just a few feet away, another person locked down here with me, but I couldn't quite make out who it was.

"Ivy?" the body croaked.

Chase.

"Oh, yes, I brought your boyfriend too," said Thana dismissively. "Anyway, this time there was a new deal. You had to be hospitalized first before we released you into the world, to work through all your little mental illnesses. Your parents' research had to undergo increased security, provided at our

That was probably just garden-variety assault. Honestly, Ivy, not everything is part of some big conspiracy."

I squinted. "You do see the irony in telling me that right now, right?"

"Not everything is about you!" Thana snapped. "See, this is why being your therapist was so annoying."

"I hate you."

"The feeling is quite mutual, I assure you. Every single week, you had *more* problems to whine about!" Thana raised the pitch of her voice to mock mine. "*Do my friends hate me? Am I going to be a huge failure when I graduate? Why do I attract creepy men at parties? What am I doing wrong? Why did Chase dump me? Is it because I'm unlovable?*" Thana sneered down at me, and my heartbeat seemed to grow louder underneath her gaze. "I'm going to be so happy when I kill you. I think about what it would feel like during every session, that is, when I'm not thinking about jamming rusty nails into my ears so that I don't have to listen to you again."

"I—" I paused. "I—" I began to laugh hysterically. "You sound so stupid!"

For the first time since I'd woken up down here, Thana didn't seem to have a response. She was gaping at me a little bit, wondering if I had finally gone over the edge.

I was still roaring with laughter. "Sorry, it's just, I've thought all of those things, word for word, repeatedly for years now! But hearing you say them aloud? They sound ridiculous! Like, you're a crazy woman who has me locked in an underground basement, and..." I momentarily lost the ability to speak through the stitches in my sides. "*This* should be a form of therapy. Everyone with anxiety should get assigned a nemesis to say their worst fears aloud, so they can hear how insane they sound."

"Your nemesis? I'm not some cartoon villain, Ivy. I'm a patriot." Thana had raised a hand, and for a moment I thought she might slap me, but she lowered it again. "I'm not surprised you're unfamiliar with patriots. If you cared about your country, you'd be more than willing to sacrifice your *third* life."

Henley spoke up from next to me. "That's not *patriotic*, that's *psychotic*. Of course Ivy isn't going to tell anyone," she asserted confidently, at the exact same moment that Chase blurted out, "The people have a right to know what you're done."

A beat of confusion was near silence as I finally began to get my laughter under control, and then Chase asked, "Seriously, who is this girl?" right as Henley said, "That's such a stupidly dangerous thing to say!"

"You can't keep secrets like this from the people you're supposed to serve," Chase protested. "Ivy or not, they're going to find out."

"The government has always kept secrets. It's safer that way," argued Henley. "Maybe *you* were unconscious while she was talking about the political ramifications of this information, or maybe you've never learned anything about the government that didn't come from a tweet, but some of us were paying attention. Ivy won't say anything because she's not stupid."

"Maybe," Chase retorted, "Ivy can decide for herself. Maybe it's not up to you."

"Maybe Ivy can speak for herself?" I added, although I didn't know who I agreed with.

"It's not up to any of you," said Thana coolly, and I realized she had walked back over to the computer while we'd been distracted. "The fate of classified data doesn't get decided by teenagers in lovers' spats. Chase and Henley weren't brought here to have opinions, they were brought here to serve as incentive."

"Incentive?" I didn't like the sound of that.

"Incentive," she repeated coolly. She began typing on the keyboard again, the sound of rapid clicking filling the room before the briefest high-pitched tone.

The pain seemed to radiate from every cell in my body, every organ. Not even my eyes were spared. I had heard of torture methods of people being pulled apart, limb from limb, but this was worse. This was being *pushed* apart from the inside out. I felt myself writhing from the agony.

The feeling stopped, and I was left dizzy and exhausted. Someone was saying something. I didn't think I was still screaming, but I couldn't be sure.

"Ivy." There were fingers snapping in front of my face. "Ivy, pay attention. You're being quite rude."

I tried to say something, but the noise that left my throat was more guttural than it was an actual word.

"Ivy, are you listening yet?"

I made another sound, and this one seemed to count as an acceptable response.

"Good. Now, I would like to limit the body count to four. I don't think it does anyone any good to involve more people, as I would have to fill out more forms, there would be a slightly bigger headline, and I'm sure it would be unfortunate for the additional parties as well."

Additional parties? Four bodies?

"No one has to die," I rasped. "I won't tell anyone."

"And now you're lying to me?" Thana *tsked*.

"I'm not!"

"Of course you are. But I already took care of it, don't worry. I took care of your professor painlessly. She barely felt a thing, and I'm willing to offer the same deal for your friends here. Well," Thana amended, "painlessly, excluding the demonstration you were just given."

Professor Whitby. Oh my god. The empty office.

Professor Whitby was dead.

I had been so stupid; I *had* told someone. I hadn't been thinking about government secrets or CIA protocol at all. I'd emailed her from my goddamn iPhone; I'd alluded to exactly what was happening. And Professor Whitby had paid the price.

"You're a horrible person." I heard Chase's groan from my right.

"I'm loyal to my *country*, Mr. Kennedy. Not to some pretty science experiment that makes my hormones act up." At the word "experiment," she looked pointedly at me.

"There's no way you were authorized to do this," said Henley, her voice remarkably steady. "I don't believe you."

"The phrase 'Better to ask forgiveness than permission' was invented for the federal government, Ms. Gara. I'm sure I'll face some sort of slap on the wrist, but if people like me didn't take bold steps, nothing would ever get done. Now, Ivy," she turned to me, "past experience indicates that if I simply kill you, your parents will find a way to bring you back."

"Don't you dare hurt them," I spat. *Were they down here somewhere too?*

"Relax, your parents are actually worth something to me. No, what I need from you is more along the lines of a DNR. Maybe a video or a letter? Something to convince them you're not *really* their daughter and they shouldn't attempt to replicate her again."

Would something like that even work?

"If I do that, then you'll let Chase and Henley go?" I attempted to negotiate.

Thana shook her head. "*No.* That's not on the table. Pay attention. If you cooperate, I won't torture them until they're bleeding out of their eyeballs."

"Seriously?" yelled Henley from my left. "What the fuck?"

"You can't be that surprised, Ms. Gara. You forfeited all of your employment perks the second you helped Ivy run away from me at that ball."

"What?" I yelled, only, it didn't sound like just my voice. It was a group of voices, familiar voices, coming from somewhere behind me.

It couldn't be.

"This," said Will, stepping forward around the metal table to stand next to me, still wearing his tux, "is a weird fucking afterparty."

CHAPTER SIXTEEN

IF—

———

Metal jammed painfully into my neck as I tried to sit up voluntarily, desperate to look behind me for my friends, or maybe desperate to turn to Henley and ask her what in god's name Thana meant by "*employment*."

"Hey, Ivy," Will said, face pinching as he took in the full sight of me, in my ballgown, lying strapped to a steel table. "Henley," he added, turning toward her. "And… whoever the fuck this guy is."

Chase scowled.

"So, what the fuck is up with this?" Will asked, facing Thana and running an anxious hand through his fluffy blond hair.

I looked back at her too and realized with a flash of panic that her hand was hovering over her gun still holstered at her hip. As she took in the rest of my friends, I had the horrible feeling she was calculating how long it would take to shoot them all.

Five against one aren't such good odds when the "one" has a gun.

"Is this why you've been acting so weird? Are you, like, a secret agent now?" Emilia asked from behind me. I couldn't decide whether to be overjoyed or horrified to see her. The second option was probably most practical, considering I had to get her out of this predicament *sans-bullet*.

I kept my focus on Thana.

"Please don't hurt them," I begged. "I'll help you figure out a DNR, or whatever, but you have to let everyone go."

"Just how stupid are you?" Thana spat, glowering at me. "Did your parents forget to grow you another brain? *You* signed their death warrant when you brought them down here." She frowned and looked back to my friends. "How exactly did you bring them here?"

I shrugged the most my restraints would allow.

"Her phone has a GPS in it, dumbass," said Aiden from behind me. I didn't think I had ever been so happy to hear him call someone a "dumbass" before. "We went to go look for her outside because she had been gone for a while and saw you putting both girls in the back of a car."

"And," cut in Rose, "we were about to get security, but we saw you flash some identification to a Secret Service agent to get passed them. So, we decided it was better to follow you ourselves."

"I bribed the Uber driver!" added Harrison. "I found one that had just dropped someone off at the ball and paid in cash so we wouldn't be tracked in the system."

My chest swelled with pride at the care my friends had taken to find me. Maybe they'd still love me after this whole ordeal after all.

Thana still looked bewildered. "How could you have tracked her phone?" she demanded. "I threw her purse into a koi pond before we left."

"Oh my god!" I gasped, overcome by excitement as I remembered. *I finally knew something the CIA didn't.* "It's because I still have my phone! My dress has pockets!"

Thana lowered her gaze to meet mine, surprise and indignation playing across her features.

"Did you just say," she growled though clenched teeth, "that your floor length, princess-skirt *ballgown* has pockets?"

I grinned. "My mom got it for me, bitch."

Thana lurched forward in a fury, and for a moment I thought she was just going to kill me with or without the DNR. Then I realized with a jolt of panic that her gun was pointed at Will. She held the weapon expertly; nothing but empty space stood between his forehead and a bullet.

"All right," she addressed my friends, her tone suddenly lacking the boiling hatred she had been directing at me. She sounded calm, professional, like we were in therapy. "If the five of you want to stay alive, I suggest you kneel down on the floor right now, palms spread out in front of you."

There was a horrific silence, and my heart froze. I couldn't see anyone but Will. I had no idea what they were thinking or might do. They didn't know the whole story—that she had already killed someone, that she would be more than willing to do it again—*Oh god. All my fault.*

Will's chest was rising and falling in a pronounced, deliberate rhythm, like he had to force himself to keep breathing; otherwise, he gave away no hint of fear as he stared back into the black hole of crazy that had once been my shrink.

Thana's eyes narrowed, and her trigger finger flexed just a fraction of an inch.

"All right," Harrison said from behind me. "We're going down. Don't shoot him."

I heard a soft shuffling and saw Thana's pupils roll downward, following the movement behind me.

Will remained upright, and I watched as Thana scrutinized him.

"What, do you think you get to be brave here?" she mocked. "That you get to play the hero because you're the one with the target on your forehead? Your generation grew up idolizing the whole 'chosen one' trope. Now you all think you can save the world, but it doesn't work like that. You're not some perfect martyr just because you'd die for your friends. To make real change, you have to stay alive. You have to be around to make the hard choices."

Her arm shifted a few degrees, down and to the left. The gun was pointing somewhere behind Will now, and I saw him stiffen.

"There," Thana said with a satisfied smile. "Now it's Alabama's life on the line instead of yours. Still feeling reckless?"

"Ma'am, I'm from Arkan—" I heard Harrison start to say before Rose cut him off with a shush.

Thana just smirked. She had won, and she knew it. Will knelt without a fight.

I knew any one of us would sacrifice themselves to save the others, just as surely as I knew none of us would let another make that choice.

Thana moved back to the computer and started typing something out with one hand, the other still aiming the gun. When finished, she sat on the desk next to the computer, crossing her legs so that neither of her feet touched the floor.

"Wha—" I began to ask before she tapped a final button and a sharp pulse swept through the room. It seemed to come from the floor; I saw Will start to spasm in the fraction of an instant before the pulse surged through the steel table to reach me. My skin tingled and my muscles felt tight, contracting reflexively. Then the pulse swept out of my body, and I fell limp.

Sore.

Ow.

Fuck.

Every part of me ached. I couldn't move. My body seemed to burn just from the thought. Why on earth would anyone ever exercise if the result felt like this?

But at least... pain meant I wasn't dead yet. Maybe there was still a way to save my friends.

Sound. Underwater?

I was too exhausted to open my eyes, so I focused all my energy toward trying to listen to the echoing noises, forcing myself to understand. It seemed like an argument, two voices.

Someone else must have woken up before me.

My brain cleared further, and I started to hear the words.

"I'm quite disappointed in you," a cool voice was saying. "Given all the exceptional work you've done throughout the rest of your internship and, of course, the beliefs you conveyed in your application essay, I thought you were a promising candidate for future work with the CIA. It's a shame, really, that you turned out to be so weak."

"I'm not weak."

"Then why did you assist that overdeveloped petri dish when she tried to get away from me at the ball?"

Okay, so that was Thana.

"What, do you think I'm stupid?" the other voice snapped. "You have higher clearance than the Secret Service, and there were dozens of agents there. There was no way we could have made it off the property; I just didn't want her to figure out that I work for you. I was only following orders."

Henley.

"Why should I believe you, Ms. Gara? You're just an intern, your orders only were to observe and report. *You* were the one who decided to befriend her."

"For the last time, I didn't *decide* to make contact. That boy forced me into his bedroom, and Ivy was close by because I was following her. *For you.* It's not my fault she saw him drag me in there, and it's not my fault she decided to come after me and break his nose. Besides, I followed your little 'emergency protocol' right afterward. I slipped both those little tablets you gave me, and the next time I saw Ivy she didn't seem to recognize me, let alone remember. I even stole her shoes so she wouldn't wake up and wonder why they were covered in blood."

Wait. Was I missing a pair of shoes?

I wished the conversation would slow down so I had time to process, but Thana was already talking again.

"That was the first time. Why did you speak to her the second time? Why were you standing together at the ball?"

Silence.

"Exactly." *Tsk.* "You really are letting me down, Ms. Gara. If I'm honest, when you initially approached her, I thought you were taking initiative, trying to collect better data. Your loyalties are clear now, however. You weren't protecting your cover when you led her away from me; you were protecting *her.*"

"It was a *mistake.* I made a bad call. Like you said, I'm an intern; I still have a lot to learn. I got caught up in the assignment, but that's all."

"Why should I believe you?"

"You read my application essay; you know what my ambitions are. Do you really think I would let teenagers stand in the way of my career?"

Another pause before the answer.

"It *would* be quite a shame to have to kill another intern; I have to fill out a special form for that. All right, I'll give you a test."

I was tired of just listening, I wanted to see what was happening. My eyelids were still heavy, but not immobile. With a great deal of effort, I managed to push them open, just in time to see Thana unlock Henley's restraints and hand her a gun.

"Kill one of the liabilities, and I'll bring you back on probation." Thana looked impassively at each of my friends, like she was trying to pick out the best piece of fruit at the supermarket. "Make it the roommate."

Henley sat up, slowly, gun in hand. She slid carefully off the table and raised the weapon, pointing it toward the floor where Emilia must have lying.

Emilia. I had never felt so helpless. I couldn't move to help her. Was there something I could say to convince Henley not to shoot? Maybe—

Henley whipped around, pointed the gun at Thana, and pulled the trigger.

Nothing happened. Oh.

Henley's gun wasn't loaded.

Thana *tsked* again and shook her head at Henley before pulling her own gun from the holster. "I told you that was a test, Ms. Gara. You failed." She fired.

Thana's gun was.

I couldn't help but shriek at the sound, so much louder than I had expected. On TV, gunshots were just a "bang," but this was an explosion. Henley fell back, out of my frame of vision.

"No!" I screamed, and I was struggling against my restraints, violently. I needed to escape, and I didn't care if I had to break my wrists to do it.

Thana walked calmly over to me and slapped me in the face.

"I hate you!" I screeched.

"The feeling is mutual," she responded calmly. "You ruined my intern."

"You're a psychopath! I'm going to gouge out your eyes and feed them to my rat!"

Wait. My rat.

"*You*," said Thana, "are going to record a video convincing your parents not to bring you back again." She knelt for a moment, out of sight, and when she appeared again her hand was soaked in blood. *Henley's blood.* "Or do I need to keep convincing you that I'm not afraid to hurt your friends?"

I shook my head. *My friends who followed me here, because I have a phone, because I have pockets.*

Thana smiled. "Wonderful. I'll be so happy when you're gone."

She walked back over to the computer and entered a sequence of keys.

My restraints snapped open.

"All right," she said, surveying the room. "I think you should stand against one of the walls. You should film the video so it only shows your face, but still, it's better to have a neutral background in case you're as bad at focusing a camera as you are at therapy."

"Fine," I said dully. I picked myself up off the table and moved sullenly next to Thana. "What else? Do you have a special CIA phone I have to film it on or something?"

She smirked at me. "Actually, since you have your phone anyway, why don't you just film it there?"

Perfect.

I put my hand in my pocket but moved my fingers past the phone and wrapped around something else. I gave a dramatic, dejected sigh, and Thana laughed.

Wow, she really hates me, I thought. Then, I lunged forward as I pulled my hand out, and I stabbed Thana in the eye with a tiny wooden hors d'oeuvres sword.

I was quite sure that maneuver would not have worked if she had ever considered me a physical threat, or if she hadn't been so caught up in my defeat, or if the CIA taught their agents to defend themselves against cheese kabobs.

Thana screamed in agony, and I tackled her, pushing her to the floor and jerking the little sword back and forth.

She wailed as her eye gave way to prosciutto and blood, and I pushed harder, trying to inflict as much damage as possible before her training kicked i—

Her hand shot forward into my stomach, and I fell off of her and landed on the floor with a grunt. She pulled the sword from her eye with another cry of pain; I used the chance to snatch her gun.

Thana shrieked incoherently when she saw the firearm and lunged forward. She was too fast. I didn't have the time to aim it, and I couldn't let her take it from me, so I went against every instinct in my body and threw it blindly away from myself as hard as I could. She didn't bother to go after it; she knew she could beat me in hand-to-hand combat.

I knew it too.

She hurled me against the wall. I could tell she was in pain, but it didn't seem to affect her concentration as much as I hoped an eye-gouging might. I wondered briefly if it was from the adrenaline or if ignoring excruciating pain was something they taught in CIA training before she smashed my head against the wall again.

At least if I die now, she won't have a reason to torture my friends anymore, I thought. I wondered what it would feel like to die. I couldn't remember either of the times I'd done it before. Maybe it didn't feel like anything at all.

Thana knocked me to the ground and grabbed the bloody hors d'oeuvre, raising it to jam in my eye.

"Hey!"

We both turned.

Henley was lying in her pool of blood, weak and shaking, but she was holding the gun.

Thana's remaining eye widened. For once, we were both surprised.

"Be careful, Ms. Gara," she said, each word slow and carefully enunciated. "Don't throw away your future for a girl. You want to be powerful, right? I can help you reach your goals—she can't."

Henley didn't flinch. "I'll be fine without you."

"She's a security threat!" Thana insisted, and I realized she was terrified. "She's barely even a person! Do the *right thing.*"

Henley let her eyes flick to me, just for a second, but when she looked back at Thana she was smiling. It was a real smile too, cheeks stretched, and eyes crinkled. She looked serene.

"I don't care about the right thing," Henley whispered, and the muscles in her index finger began to flex. "I care about her."

An explosion sounded from the gun. I felt hot blood pour over me.

Thana dropped to the ground. Her once-twisted face now fell slack, and her one remaining eye stared open, unseeing.

Thana was dead at last.
And I was still alive.

EPILOGUE

The world around us is full of light. The sky is painted with the palest shade of blue, and sunbeams glint off piles of half-melted snow.

I am sitting across from my parents at a stone table in the center of an outdoor courtyard. We've been silent for five minutes; no one seems to know quite what to say. My mom's eyebrows are pressed upward, and her eyes are wide as she analyzes my face and body language. My dad's brows do the opposite and pinch down into his lashes, a familiar expression that means he's deep in thought.

I decide this means it's my job to break the ice, if only because I'm on a bit of a tight schedule today, and I think that Whiskey is starting to get a little chilly inside of my dress pocket.

"So," I say, and they both straighten up to listen before I realize I didn't really have anything to say. *Hmm.*

It's been weeks since Thana died, but it's the first time I've seen either of them. Henley called one of her CIA supervisors to report what had happened—before, of course, she would let us call 911 for her—and a team of agents came to collect us.

We had been kept in a windowless "observation room" for two days while they determined that we could be discrete enough to be released before they came up with a real plan, but my parents had been taken in to be questioned about Thana, my memories, and the science behind it all for multiple weeks.

Henley is still healing but out of the hospital, and as far as I know we're going to be allowed to sign non-disclosure forms or something of the like rather than, well, dying.

But now I am talking to the people who made me three separate times, and I can't think of anything that captures what I want to say. I fall back on a classic way to diffuse tension: a horrible joke.

"Is the hospital going to start giving out punch cards? Like, die three times, get a free slice of cafeteria pie?"

Dad gives me a pity laugh.

"So, we're joking about this?" my mom asks. "You're not…" She doesn't want to finish the sentence.

"Oh, I am," I say, because I know what she means anyway. "I was so angry, and then I was scared, and I've been confused since 2020, but…" I bite my right thumb nail. "But I don't know what else to say. I don't totally know how I feel about having, you know, died. But I'm still in a better place than I used to be, and someday I'll be in a better place than I am now."

"We wanted to tell you," my dad says. "But we weren't allowed; it was part of the contract we made to save your life. And we didn't know that woman would—"

"I know," I interrupt. "I don't know if I would have made the same choice for myself, but I know why you made it, and I know that it's already done, and… and I love you guys. A lot."

"We love you too," my mom says through tears. "We couldn't lose you, Ivy."

And I'm crying too.

"I'm so sorry that I haven't been open with you and that I wasn't really that nice to you during high school," I say. "If it helps, I don't think it was a clone thing; I think it was a teenage and depression thing, but I loved you the whole time."

My parents smile and nod through their tears.

"I know," sobs my mom.

I know my relationship won't be magically perfect now. We'll still bicker sometimes, or miscommunicate, or keep things from each other the way teenagers and parents sometimes do. But I don't think I'll ever feel quite so isolated from them, like I did during high school and the beginning of this year. I think it will be easier, now that I understand them and understand how much they love me.

I reach my hand across the table, and they both reach out to hold it.

"Can I make a suggestion for the punch card?" my mom asks. "I don't think you should get pie. Maybe angel food cake?"

I snort at the terrible joke, and she looks playfully offended.

"What, it wasn't funny? Has that joke been beaten to death?"

My dad and I laugh together at that.

We stay there talking, joking, and holding hands until my phone pings with a notification from my schedule, reminding me that I need to leave.

As we hug goodbye, I whisper "I love you guys," one more time before I go to meet my friends.

***

When I told Henley my friends were helping me throw my own "funeral," her eyes lit up and she said, "Oh! Like Mark Twain, right?"

I nodded and smiled as I handed her a glossy black invitation, because I didn't want to admit that I had actually taken the idea from an episode of *Vampire Diaries*. Either way, it seemed like a good idea. I wanted to mourn my previous selves, to acknowledge their existence, and their loss, before I began to move on.

So now I'm leaving my parents to walk down to the waterfront where my friends, Chase, and Henley were already waiting. I am alone on the sidewalk in my funeral attire: a tight black dress, black boots, and a black fascinator I bought to seem extra serious. I look entirely funeral ready.

My friends begin to set up bouquets of flowers and sheets of black ribbon to tribute my old lives. They are in the room we are renting at a bar near the Potomac, and Henley got the owner to leave us bottles of champagne and mojito ingredients.

Aiden, who is the most Catholic in the group, is searching out an appropriate hymn for the service. Emilia is furiously scribbling on a sheet of paper as she tries to perfect her toast. Will is pouring drinks for us while Harrison divides up slices of cake. Chase is pinning up photos of my past self. It's going to be an amazing funeral.

But I'm not going to make it. A black car with tinted windows is pulling up next to me, a boy I recognize is getting out, and I'm not fast enough to get away.

I'm not at my funeral to see the photo board or taste the cake, to sing Aiden's hymn or hear Emilia's toast.

I am fourteen blocks away, lying motionless on a black leather seat as the car races out of town. I am alone, heading unwillingly into the unknown, and only Whiskey is there to squeak in protest as a boy secures my body in the back of the car and mumbles in a European accent, "See? I told you I only needed to drop something off at my car."

ACKNOWLEDGMENTS

———

Thank you very much for reading *If*. I had so much fun writing it, and I hope you had fun reading it too! This was my first novel, and I could not have created it without an incredible amount of hard work and support from my family, my friends, and my team at New Degree Press, especially my amazing editors, Kristin and Erika!

Additionally, I would like to give special thanks to the following friends, family, and fans who helped support me while I created this story:

Amber Gerdes

Amina Sadural

Amy Fernandes

Anjali Goradia

Ann Viozzi

Anna Gross

Annalee Atkinson

Ashley Hall

Ben Zeller

Brendan Wilder

Brian McCrann

Carol L. Gross

Caroline Pritchard

Charleen McCready

Daisy Steinthal

Elizabeth Williams

Eric Bazail-Eimil

Eric Koester

Gregory Bernstein

Isabel Field

Isabel Janovsky

Jarrett Schneider

Jessica Lee

Jim and Marian Dyck

Juan Camilo Gonzalez
Julie Pritchard
Kari Pritchard
Katherine Eu
Katherine McLellan
Katherine Williamson
Katie Burford
Kelsey Bryson
Kyle Alexander
Lance Guthrie
Lily Howard
Lucy Sonsalla
Maddy Mitchell
Magdalena Paz
Maren P. Wilder
Maria Howard
Mary Barton-Rau
Matthew Failor
Melissa Sabatino
Michael Newport
Molly Summers

Naresh and Sunita Nayar
Nathan Barber
Nicholas Young
Nicole Bryce
Nirvana Khan
O'Meara Riley
Rachel Stinson
Rebecca Stene and Renee
Allbright
Robert Wilder
Sara Holmes
Shreya Nayar and Carlos
Gonzalez
Siarah Romero
Sophia Belhumer
Stephen Robert Hays
Suzannah Mazur
Sydney Gilbert
Taylor Battey
Yasmine Robinson
Zev Burton